SOCIAL THEORY AND ECONOMIC CHANGE

Social Theory and Economic Change

MICHAEL ARGYLE · REINHARD BENDIX
M.W. FLINN · EVERETT E. HAGEN

Edited by Tom Burns and S. B. Saul

TAVISTOCK PUBLICATIONS

distributed in the United States
by BARNES & NOBLE, Inc.

First published in 1967
by Tavistock Publications Limited
11 New Fetter Lane, London EC4
and printed in Great Britain
in 11 pt Monotype Imprint, one point leaded
by Cox & Wyman Ltd
London, Reading, and Fakenham

Distribution in the United States of America
by Barnes & Noble, Inc.

Contributions to the
Seminar on the Theory of Economic Change
held at the University of Edinburgh in March 1965

University of Edinburgh
Faculty of Social Sciences Staff Seminars
Report No. 1

Contents

v

Editors' Note

The four papers published in this short book were read to a Seminar organized by the Faculty of Social Sciences at Edinburgh University and held at the end of the spring term 1965. We should like to record our indebtedness to the authors of the papers and to the many distinguished people from this country and abroad who attended the Seminar and enriched its proceedings.

The central theme of the Seminar was Professor Hagen's views on the process of social change as expressed in his book *On the Theory of Social Change* and elaborated further in the paper presented by him to the Seminar. The papers appear in the order in which they were given to the Seminar and are prefaced by a short review in which the organizers attempt to outline some of the main lines of criticism offered in the course of the discussions.

Introduction

TOM BURNS AND S. B. SAUL

If history is to be more than narrative, then it has to explain. Even as narrative, the historian's selection and ordering of events and attitudes, of successful and unsuccessful actions, of speech and writings can be meaningful only if he observes a set of principles by which he selects and orders. If history, in short, is to be something other, and more, than news, then it is a search for explanation. Historical explanation is a process of simplification, by which a great many diverse things are shown to be connected or similar. This purpose demands that events are shown to be causally connected and, moreover, that the causal principles themselves are ordered according to some hierarchic system. It is in this sense that Collingwood regarded history as a science.

To adduce a multiplicity of causal factors without relating them to each other either burkes the historian's task or, more seriously, misleads by assuming that causes are unconnected with each other and therefore additive: i.e. that the *more* causes one can find, the better the explanation. The openness of British eighteenth-century society, the freedom with which business associations were entered into with friends and friends of friends or with fellow sectarians, and the wide diffusion through the ranks of society of the perception by early scientists that natural events 'obeyed' natural laws: all three generalizations have entered into discussion of the 'causes' of the Industrial Revolution. Putting them into juxtaposition suggests some logical and empirical link between them. But, if one exists, do not such 'causes' merely operate as dependent variables? Are the three 'causes' (or effects) in fact similar? If so, is there some underlying social, economic, or political factor which 'explains' the coexistence of similar dispositions in these different sectors of eighteenth-century society?

Can one rest at the point at which, for example, Landes stops in his brilliant essay on the Industrial Revolution (in Volume VI of the *Cambridge Economic History of Europe*) with an enumeration of the institutional factors, economic and social, that were *concomitant* with the economic and technical changes that occurred in Britain during the critical seventy years of the Industrial Revolution?

The force of the dilemma is perhaps more compelling, or more apparent, in economic history than in political or military history, where, it is said 'most historians are content to leave to the social scientists the attempt to formulate general laws' and where 'the emphasis now is upon the satisfaction of a disinterested curiosity about the past'. In economic history, curiosity takes less deprecatory forms.

Of course, to make sense of such a question as 'Why did the Industrial Revolution occur at the time, and in the place, it did?' is to commit oneself to a bold and possibly presumptuous endeavour. But it is towards such endeavours that the whole of economic history is directed: towards the reduction of the infinitude of historical facts by ordering them in terms of explanatory principles – the fewer the better.

Hagen's 'status-withdrawal' hypothesis was, therefore, welcomed by the economic historians at the conference because it might conceivably provide some general explanatory model of the change from traditional to industrial societies, which is at present conspicuously lacking. Hagen gave in a preliminary paper an outline sketch of the general theory that he proposes as an answer – admittedly primitive and incomplete – to certain fundamental questions:

'Therefore, taking as our analytical model the unreal case of the *perfectly* traditional state, in which government is completely authoritarian and techniques are unchanging, we may ask: Why have societies tended to approximate to this model? What forces have caused temporary departures from this typical state? And what forces have caused return to it? These questions, I suggest, are vital ones in any theory of social change.'

The first condition which must exist, to explain the persistence for a long time of authoritarian government, is this: the people of the society must be content with it.

He goes on to equate traditional with authoritarian societies, and invokes psycho-analytical theory to suggest that child-rearing practices in traditional societies tend to develop the kind of character that avoids facing the possibility of changing normal lines of action, 'and when the perception of a problem cannot be avoided' quiets anxiety 'by relying on someone else's judgement'. The closed circle of authoritarian stability and decision-avoiding dependency that can result leads to a kind of equilibrium which is self-perpetuating.

However, 'in life there are always factors which may disturb the equilibrium'. In particular, the ruling elite may act too oppressively or offensively for the lower orders (especially those immediately below them) to continue to feel the deference and dependence that are essential to the maintenance of the system. It is in these circumstances that 'withdrawal of status respect' occurs.

The consequences for the social system make themselves felt over a long period of time, but are, in any case, the operative factors in inducing a need for achievement among a sufficiently large proportion of people not born to elite status to create, eventually, major social changes – of many kinds, it should be said, and not merely those that concern the initiation of fundamentally different rates of economic growth, or technological progress, or political evolution. Hagen concludes:

'The hypothesized effects, then, are these: Among the adults of the first generation of lesser elite so affected, the reaction is anger or irritation (depending on the degree of severity of the derogation) and anxiety. These reactions constitute no change in personality but only one in behaviour in response to changed circumstances. However, the children of these adults, seeing that their parents' role in life causes anxiety, do not find it a fully satisfying model, as previous generations did. Alternative social roles are, in general, not open to these children, for a variety of objective and emotional reasons, and so they respond by somewhat repressing within themselves their parents' values without acquiring others. They do not have *any* role values with the clarity and intensity their parents did. The process, I suggest, is cumulative for several successive generations, and in, say, the third or fourth generation there appears pronounced norm-lessness (shiftlessness, anomie, or, in Merton's term, retreatism).

There is reason to suspect that retreatism affects men more

than women because of the differences between the social roles of the sexes. After several generations, then, there will appear men who are retreatists and weak, but women who are less so. Reacting to the ineffectiveness of their husbands, the women will desire intensely that their sons shall be more effective, and will respond with delight to each achievement in infancy and boyhood. That is, infantile and childhood initiative and problem-solving will be emotionally rewarding rather than anxiety-creating.

What more can be said about the personality of these creative individuals? (1) In the most common case, since they trust their own judgements when facing new problems, they will wish to participate in political decisions, and will reject authoritarian government and move for representative government. The presence of such individuals here and there throughout the population is probably a necessary condition for the appearance of representative government. (2) Rather than use their creative abilities to rise to the social roles of the higher elites, they will reject close identification with those roles, both because of their anger at those elites and because accepting the social values of those elites would involve admitting their own little worth, since those elites think of them as of little worth. (3) They will, however, be possessed of gnawing, burning desire to prove themselves (to themselves, as well as to their fellows and the higher elites). Hence they will seek roles in which they can do so, and often ones in which they can gain power and status relative to the higher elites. Being creative, they will be quite ready and willing to create new roles.

What they turn to will be determined in part by the models of effective and satisfying behaviour they find during their childhood somewhere in their history or their folklore, and in part by the opportunities open to them. In the modern world, to many creative individuals in socially rebellious groups in traditional societies no other road to power, recognition, and proof to oneself of one's ability will seem as inviting as economic prowess, and many such creative individuals will become economic innovators. In the cases of England, Japan, and Colombia, which I have examined in some detail, such groups have provided a disproportionate share of the leaders in the transition to economic growth.'

These quotations from what is already a brief sketch of a very elaborate thesis cannot hope to do it justice, but may serve as a preface to Hagen's paper, which is by way of being a postscript to his book.

The personality hypothesis can certainly be made to look persuasive for some contemporary industrializing countries, and, as Flinn showed, probably has some relevance when applied to the Industrial Revolution in Britain. Psychology shows that 'need for achievement' is a distinct and analysable feature of the personality, and the hypothesis does provide some evidence for features which historical individuals might have shared – Woodrow Wilson and Luther were cited. The approach is stimulating and exciting, and obviously brings out a significant element in the process of historical change.

There are, however, certain fundamental difficulties. The hypothesis as it was presented by Hagen is too vague to be falsifiable; it assumes contrast conceptions (traditional/industrial societies, etc.) which are not, in fact, exclusive. And although such contrast conceptions are, as Bendix says, 'indispensable as a first orientation', they 'should not be mistaken for analysis'. Indeed, relied on for more than the crudest initial service, they can be misleading. Most societies that have been studied factually, however remote or stagnant, show that innovating activity is present. Hagen never established his starting-point of traditional society in Europe, and, indeed, present thinking about European history stresses change, not stagnation. In any case, the innovator may lose his struggle against traditional forces. To give the Hagen approach historical usefulness it is necessary to give at least as much attention to what it is that must be changed and the forces that must be overcome. This much is evident from the argument underlying Hagen's paper, which seems to suggest that English society was potentially innovative from the twelfth century on; his paper, in effect, puts the whole question of the timing of the transition from pre-industrial Britain to modern industrialized society back where it was.

Then there is the question of giving consideration to the variety of forms that entrepreneurship has taken in different times and places, especially with the mounting complexity of the modern world. Does the would-be innovator, simply because of the urge that is driving him, find it possible to equip himself with the other characteristics necessary for success? Have we all the same potential to be realized under favourable conditions? May it not be that there are important differences between the motivations of the inventor-scientist and those of the entrepreneur. The theory seems to make no radical distinction: both types of men are the product of the same child-rearing practices. But the entrepreneur may well have to be a more callous individual, little concerned with susceptibilities. Moreover, two or more men of different personality may combine in a partnership and thus achieve maximum effectiveness. What of Schumpeter's notion that innovation itself can become institutionalized, with science and technology entering upon an almost independent existence?

Historically, too, the Freudian element seemed to rest upon a slight basis. Groups, such as nation-states, are not sufficiently coherent and integrated to have as rigid a pattern of child-rearing as is required. Flinn showed this in his paper, and available evidence suggests not only wide variations within groups, but changes from generation to generation. Furthermore, though the basis of this theory is that of individual case-studies and Freudian psychology with a time-scale essentially of two or three generations, Hagen has sought to translate or aggregate this to cover total societies and encompass up to twenty generations. This means, then, that he is, in fact, speaking simply in metaphor and there is no longer scientific content to it. An absolute dichotomy results – a universal hypothesis in theory on the one hand, and simple narrative sequences on the other.

A major problem for historians will always be that of collecting evidence. Here, great appreciation was expressed for Flinn's most original and stimulating paper. Some reservations were noted: one related again to the homogeneity of child-rearing practices within any group, and inevitably the question arose whether the prominence of certain non-conformist groups in the Industrial Revolution could not effectively be explained by more old-fashioned arguments, such as their legal exclusion from other forms of activity. Scepticism was felt over Flinn's argument that certain educational groups deliberately prepared children for their future role in the new industrial society. Many of these groups appealed to industrialists, among others, for financial help, and their public statements were likely to be geared towards what they imagined their patrons would like to hear rather than to be expressions of actual policy. Nevertheless, it was felt that the paper represented a significant step forward.

There are, however, further dimensions of difficulty besides the lack of direct evidence. Many of the hypotheses of social sciences are born from within a certain institutional structure and have significance, not autonomously, but only within the particular set of assumptions, the particular context, both institutional and cultural, which saw their birth. Their applicability in a different societal context (different in a spatial and a time dimension) fades. For example, judged against present-day norms, cruelties involved with child-upbringing in the seventeenth and eighteenth centuries could be said to have certain effects, if conclusions were drawn from parallels with case-histories documented in the twentieth century. But general cultural norms in the seventeenth century were so brutalized compared with those of our own day, and standards of expectation and anticipation so different, that it is quite impossible to say whether the psychological reactions of children then to these actions would be similar to those in twentieth-century case-histories of cruelty. Should one therefore try to judge the effects according to a rule that *relatively* greater cruelty meted out to a child, beyond the prevailing norms of the seventeenth century, would have a similar effect to *relatively* greater cruelty judged against twentieth-century standards, rather than compare absolute facts of treatment in the seventeenth and the twentieth century? Does the differing consciousness about cruelty matter? If it does, then how is the historian to try to measure individual case-histories in a remote period against a 'norm' for that period which he has no scientific means of measuring? The problems created by translating hypotheses and means of measuring and testing them against a time dimension are profound.

In general, there was a feeling that the economic historian had in the past been drawing his hypotheses too heavily from economic theory and that there was room for equivalent reception of new ideas from other disciplines. Argyle's paper certainly made one aware of new kinds of relationship for the historian to be on the look-out for. Many of those to which he made reference had direct relevance to ideas and relationships involved in writing about a single person, a single firm, or a single family – as far as context is concerned – and about one or two generations – as far as time-scale is concerned. It was more problematical whether one could use the ideas as effectively, whether they had as much authority and relevance, when seeking to analyse a more complex, wider context of change – such as an industry, a region, or an economy – and changes over a much longer time-scale.

The general tenor of Bendix's contribution, indeed, was to criticize the feasibility of universalistic explanations of social change – not because of any failings in the particular theory under discussion, or in any previous attempts, but because such explanations necessarily involved ignoring the historical experience of societies and dealing with social structures in a 'before-and-after' sense. While this might be necessary for any particular attempt at historical explanation, one also needed to redress the tendency towards reification that entered with this kind of verbal manipulation. It was necessary to keep in mind the processual, dynamic properties of historical societies – the actions that kept them in being – and to develop adequate analytical models by which they could relieve or complement the static forms to which thinking in terms of systems lent itself. By basing the analysis of social change on comparative studies of a limited kind one could avoid the pitfalls that come from highlighting the contrasts of 'before-and-after' structures: 'Emphasis may be placed on the persistent distinctiveness of the Western experience which is as notable in its feudal traditions as in its modern industrialism and democracy.'

It was significant, however, that a good deal of time was spent during the conference in establishing a mutual discourse rather than in carrying it on. This was probably because psychologists and others have been asking and answering their questions in contexts other than those which are normally used by economic historians – even with regard to such concepts as 'leadership', 'entrepreneurship', 'innovation', and 'social change' itself – and an effort might be usefully made in the future to discuss the whole matter of terminology more extensively.

Social Theory
and the Industrial Revolution

M. W. FLINN

Social theory, and the Industrial Revolution in Britain, are both very broad themes: to attempt to relate them within the compass of a single paper is either extremely presumptuous or excessively foolhardy. In either case I shall not be able to avoid the charge of superficiality. The very recent nature of the work in this field by Hagen and others has allowed little time as yet for comfortable digestion, and one of the peculiar difficulties of this no-man's-land between complementary disciplines is that many of its propositions are not susceptible to the normal processes of historical verification. Moreover, I take it to be the function of a seminar paper to offer for discussion some tentative speculations rather than to put forward a thesis from which every unprovable assertion has been quietly eliminated, or in which every generalization is so fully proven as to admit of no further discussion. Any conclusions suggested in this paper must necessarily, therefore, be more than usually tentative.

I must say at the outset that the aspect of the Industrial Revolution with which I am going to be concerned in this paper is not its course or its consequences, but its origins. Not until Ashton wrote his little book on *The Industrial Revolution* in 1948 did any historian appear to give serious consideration to the question of the origins of the Industrial Revolution. Before then, for the most part, two types of generalization took the place of a genuinely analytical approach. The first generation of economic historians, covering the period from the publication of Toynbee's *Lectures* to the First World War, were too fascinated by the wonder of the Industrial Revolution and by what seemed to them its tragic consequences to spare more than a few superficial generalizations about origins, and embraced fairly indiscriminately the influence of ideas like

B   9

laissez-faire, the role of an expanding trading empire, and, above all, technological advance. The second generation, trailing a long way behind a vanguard led by Mantoux, reacted against the cataclysmic school by observing the continuity of economic development in eighteenth-century Britain. A fine batch of studies in the interwar period, both general and sectoral, established this continuity so successfully that the very conception of an Industrial Revolution was in imminent danger of death by neglect, until it was rescued by the unerring common sense of Ashton.

These approaches to the origins of the Industrial Revolution were, of course, complementary, and remain valid, if partial, contributions to an understanding of the problem. That they were only partial explanations has been emphasized by postwar development in the theoretical and empirical study of economic growth. The awakening of interest in the analysis of economic growth after the Second World War is to be explained by a combination of many factors – the pioneering work of Lundberg, Schumpeter, Colin Clark, and Harrod; profound dissatisfaction with the social and economic consequences of the stagnation of the interwar years; the urgent need to breathe new economic life into the shattered wildernesses of Europe's extensive war-zones; and, above all, the new-found desire of the world's underdeveloped countries and ex-colonial territories to make a start on the long journey towards Western standards of affluence. The response to these pressures has been a burgeoning of theories of economic growth.

Economic historians have, however, been slow to avail themselves of the conceptual equipment the economists have been forging in the past score of years. Nevertheless, a start has been made, and at last, in the 1960s, people are beginning to ask of the Industrial Revolution: Why did it happen? Why did it happen first in Britain? And why did it happen when it did? As a consequence of some purposeful rethinking by Habakkuk, Deane and Cole, Rostow, and others, allied to a vigorous scraping of the statistical barrel, it is already becoming a great deal more possible than it was, say, when Ashton wrote his *Industrial Revolution*, to scrutinize, on a strictly *economic* plane, the process of growth in the eighteenth-century economy. This is not to say that we are within striking distance of success, or that we shall ever have anything like the wealth of relatively precise material on which historians of the late nineteenth and twentieth centuries can draw; but at least we are better placed than we were twenty years ago.

But the more we become able to focus attention on economic variables in eighteenth-century developments – on demand at home and abroad, on population growth, on the supply of capital, on the provision of the basic social overheads, and on technology as it affected the production function – the more apparent it becomes that there are some pieces missing from the jigsaw. However the changes are rung on the strictly economic variables, they can never quite be made to add up to a convincing explanation of the initiation or acceleration of economic growth.

If this discovery is disappointing, there is nothing new or surprising in it. Economic theorists, who are used, as Domar (1957, p. 22) points out, to 'snatching from the enormous and complex mass of facts called reality a few, simple, easily manageable key points which, when put together in some cunning way, become for certain purposes a substitute for reality itself', have long been consciously consigning to the limbo of *ceteris paribus* the greater part of the whole range of non-economic variables with which Arthur Lewis, for example, was extensively concerned. Rostow's analysis of *The Stages of Economic Growth*, for instance, gives considerable prominence to non-economic factors in growth. I need only remind you that his 'pre-conditions' stage required that '*the idea* spreads not merely that economic progress is possible, but that economic progress is a necessary condition for some other purpose, judged to be good: be it national dignity, private profit, the general welfare, or a better life for the children ... *New types of enterprising men come forward*' (Rostow, 1960, p. 6; italics added). As McClelland (1961, p. 337) says, 'the shortest way to achieve economic objectives might turn out to be through changing people first'.

The non-economic factors that have so far most attracted the interest of economic historians, or that seem most relevant to a study of the origins of the Industrial Revolution, fall into three broad categories. The first considers the social environment within which entrepreneurs operate: it is an approach that sees increases in entrepreneurial and innovational activity as resulting, on the one hand, from changes in the degree of tolerance accorded to deviance from the traditional norms of entrepreneurial behaviour and, on the other, from changing attitudes to economic tasks in a

broad social context. The second recognizes that, while entrepreneurship is a factor vital to any acceleration in the rate of
economic growth, it is not the *only* social factor involved in the
process of industrialization; the reverse of this coin is the con-
ditioning of a labour force to the discipline of all that is involved in
modern industrial organization with a high degree of division of
labour. The third concerns the actual capacity of society to produce industrial leaders – entrepreneurs and inventors – and involves consideration of factors influencing the quality – the energy
and innovational capacity – of entrepreneurs, as well as the
number of potential entrepreneurial types as a proportion of the
total population.

Much of the work that has been channelled into the first of these
three directions rests on theoretical foundations laid by Ralph
Linton in the 1930s and Talcott Parsons in the postwar period
(Linton, 1936; Parsons, 1951; Parsons & Shils, 1952). It has led
over the past dozen years or so (principally at the Harvard Research Center in Entrepreneurial History (see Aitken, 1965, pp.
3–19)) to discussion of two sets of analytical concepts in the
context of economic development. The first of these evaluates the
significance for economic growth of the Parsonian pattern variables,
or at least of the three that Hoselitz (1960, pp. 23–51) has suggested
are most relevant to the analysis of growth – the switch from
ascriptive to achieved status, from universalism to particularism
in the distribution among performers of economically relevant
tasks, and from specificity to diffuseness in the performance of
these tasks. The second attempts to assess the importance of the
changing relationship between entrepreneurs and the society in
which they operate, a relationship in which particular social *roles*
are circumscribed by traditional sets of *sanctions*. Cultural norms
determine the limits of action by establishing for each individual
or class of individuals a role. Individual behaviour is circumscribed
by other people's expectations of what is normal for that role.
'When an individual's behavior in fulfilling a role', says Cochran
(1949, p. 153) of the Harvard Center, 'such as father or business
executive, accords closely with the conceptions of the role held by
people in general, he can be regarded as fulfilling a normal or stable
social role.' Society delineates and circumscribes that role by a
series of sanctions designed to discourage deviance. But since no
two people will react in exactly the same way to given cultural

norms, there can be no rigid pattern of role performance – rather a broad band, the limits of which are set by role expectations. Thus some deviance is to be expected in all role performance, but the sanctions determine that the deviance is minor and without lasting social effects. Sanctions may take two basic forms. *Formal* sanctions are those that society prescribes legally or institutionally. The medieval Church's condemnation of usury was not merely an exhortation – as such it would have been even more ineffective in discouraging deviance than it was – it was, of course, a sanction enforced by the ecclesiastical courts. *Informal* sanctions are those enforced by social opinions and attitudes. Thus, as an extreme example, a trade union might send a member to Coventry for some deviance which did not fall within the scope of its proscriptive regulations; or, in the eighteenth century, the Quakers would cut off from membership a Friend who had deviated to the extent of going bankrupt, a form of sanction experienced, for instance, by Charles Lloyd, uncle of Sampson Lloyd, the founder of the bank, in the 1720s.

There is little doubt, I am sure, that these theoretical approaches can prove valuable in the study of *some* key points of economic history both in dissecting the interrelationship between social change and economic growth and in explaining the initiation of changes in the rate of growth. But I think that their usefulness is limited to *some* situations – that these particular social changes do not necessarily occur in every major economic advance. The problem of implanting growth into stagnant, or near-stagnant, traditional societies involves, certainly, in addition to all the machinery of accumulation, the strategy of investment, and the crashing of the population barrier, a social revolution which may be well described in these conceptual terms. The future historian of the countries that are now, in the mid-twentieth century, struggling to create 'the conditions of economic progress' will certainly find this conceptual framework an essential aid to his analysis of take-off. But I am less sure that the historian of Britain's Industrial Revolution will necessarily find the same weapons equally suited to his needs. This disappointing conclusion arises, I think, largely because the British Industrial Revolution was unique in being the first industrial revolution. All subsequent ones differed in being able to import, if they so wished, new industrial techniques as well as actual capital from Britain or other advanced countries, in addition to being able to learn the advantages of new forms of organization and effective economic policies in the most painless manner. Inevitably, the British experience of Rostow's pre-conditions stage was more prolonged and gradual than that pre-ceding most subsequent industrial revolutions. It is only required, for example, that the necessary 'dichotomous choices' of the Parsonian system should have occurred *before* the industrial revolution. The gradual nature of the British development would allow these social changes to have occurred in a period remote from the take-off. They may, in other words, have occurred, say, as an aspect of the transition from Rostow's traditional society to his pre-conditions stage, rather than of the transition from the pre-conditions to the take-off. Since I am confining myself to the social environment of the take-off, I am less certain that these particular, no doubt important, social changes are immediately relevant to the British Industrial Revolution.

The second of the broad categories of non-economic factors I referred to involves changing the social attitudes of labour. For it is unlikely that a society, however vigorously led by entrepreneurs, will advance rapidly and comfortably along the road to industrialization unless it can at the same time persuade a labour force, hitherto accustomed to the freedom and flexibility of a mainly agricultural, craft, or domestic way of life, to fall easily and un-protestingly into the discipline and rigidity of large-scale industrial organization. There is, I would suggest, some evidence that an adjustment of this nature was consciously premeditated and vigor-ously instilled into the labouring generations of the eighteenth century, both before and during the period of the Industrial Revolution.

Some form of mass education for the working classes first began to be provided at the beginning of the eighteenth century; and throughout this century and into the early nineteenth century, the Charity and Sunday Schools were the principal channels through which the middle and upper classes sought to impose their social ideas upon the working class. It might not be too serious an exaggeration to claim that these schools represented the most significant or influential new force being brought to bear on the social attitudes of a large section of the labouring population during the eighteenth century. For this reason, the aims and ideology of these schools may have some bearing upon the undoubted fact of the creation of an industrial labour force which submitted itself peaceably enough to the socially disturbing rigours of urbanization and industrialization to a degree, for example, that permitted the proprietors of the Stockport Sunday School to comment in the year of the Blanketeers March – 'Our labouring poor demeaned themselves with a propriety of conduct well-according with their situation. The patient and silent resignation with which they sustained hunger and nakedness, even in the face of a rigorous winter, amidst declining wages and the advance [in the price] of provisions is fresh in every recollection.'[1]

How was this 'silent resignation' achieved? An interesting train of social thinking is discernible in the minds of those who provided the Charity and Sunday Schools. It started with the belief in a close correlation between ignorance and crime. While the mid-twentieth century may be less happy about this correlation, there is little doubt that a belief in the virtues of education in preventing lawlessness, in taming the social rebel, was a powerful influence behind the Charity and Sunday School movements. 'The State', asserted no less than Adam Smith (1776), 'derives no inconsiderable advantage from [the instruction of the common people]. The more they are instructed, the less liable they are to the delusions of enthusiasm and superstition, which, among ignorant nations, frequently occasion the most dreadful disorders. An instructed and intelligent people besides, are always more decent and orderly than an ignorant and stupid one.' Commenting more practically upon the foundation of a Sunday School in Leeds in 1784, the *Gentleman's Magazine* (Vol. LIV, p. 177) observed that 'this institution wears a most promising appearance, and, were it to be adopted generally, would do more towards lessening the increase of felons than all the schemes that have been proposed'.

More specifically, however, with a view to the needs of an industrializing society, the merits of Charity School education went further in the direction of effecting the inculcation of the essential virtues of submission and obedience in the labouring people. 'We may lay this down as an incontestible truth', stated Beilby Porteus, Bishop of London towards the end of the century, 'that a well-informed and intelligent people, more particularly a people well acquainted with the sacred writings, will always be more orderly, more decent, more humane, more virtuous, more

1. Annual Report of the Stockport Sunday School (Stockport, 1817).

religious, more obedient to their superiors, than a people totally devoid of all instruction and all education.'[1] The role of Charity Schools, according to Isaac Watts, writing in the 1720s, was 'to impress upon their tender minds . . . the duties . . . of humility and submission to superiors',[2] a sentiment echoed by Philip Doddridge in one of his children's hymns of the 1740s:

> *To those whom He hath cloath'd with power,*
> *I should be subject every hour.*
> *To parents, and to rulers, too,*
> *Pay honour and obedience due.*[3]

There was a sharp contrast between the ideals of Charity and Sunday School education in the eighteenth century and the goals of social mobility implied in the Mechanics' Institute movement of the 1820s or Samuel Smiles's 'Self-Help' of the mid-nineteenth century. The Charity and Sunday Schools were intended very clearly to strengthen the educational barriers between classes. The balance between an education sufficient to inculcate a due sense of obedience and humility, and an absence of social or economic aspirations, on the one hand, and one likely to promote a desire for social climbing, on the other, was a fine one, but the providers of the Charity and Sunday Schools did not flinch from drawing such a distinction, and from opting unhesitatingly for the former. 'As the children of the rich in general', wrote Isaac Watts, 'ought to enjoy such an education as may fit them for the better businesses of life, so the children of the poor . . . should not be generally educated in such a manner as may raise them above the services of a lower station.'[4] Accordingly, the Stockport Sunday School of the 1780s claimed modestly that 'all that we have in view is to qualify young persons of both sexes for various useful and practical arts';[5] and it opened its premises 'for the reception of poor children of all denominations and descriptions, who are to be instructed in

---

1. Beilby Porteus, *Charges to the clergy* (1786), quoted by Dugald Stewart, *Works*, Vol. VIII, p. 51.
2. Isaac Watts, *An essay towards the encouragement of Charity Schools* (1728, p. vi).
3. Philip Doddridge, *Divine songs, or the principles of the Christian religion* (1744, p. 35). See also Phyllis J. Wetherell (1950).
4. Isaac Watts, *An essay towards the encouragement of Charity Schools* (1728, p. 14).
5. Annual Report of the Stockport Sunday School (Stockport, 1806).

those branches of learning suitable to their station in life'.[1]

But the aims of these schools were even more explicitly geared to the manning of the growing industries. As the Committee of the Manchester Sunday Schools expressed it later in the eighteenth century (cf. Wadsworth, 1950–51, p. 300), the Sunday Schools 'called in a sense of religious obligation to the aid of industry' – 'that most desirable union', as Bishop Porteus declared in 1786, 'of manual labour and spiritual instruction'.[2] William Brooke, the organizer of Sunday Schools in Bath, praised 'the advantage [the children] derive from thus being regularly assembled together on a stated day in each week – they become reconciled to confinement, and are habituated to behave with silence and respect in the presence of their superiors'.[3] The Stockport Sunday School Committee neatly summarized the issue: 'Are the proprietors of manufactories desirous of obtaining honest and industrious servants? Let them require a sound character, as indispensably requisite for their engagement, and the youth of both sexes will, by availing themselves of a Sunday School education . . . seek to possess this necessary qualification.'[4]

In the last resort, however, it was, of course, a willingness and capacity to work hard for long hours that mattered, and the Charity and Sunday Schools were geared most directly to meet this need. 'Industry is the great principle of duty that ought to be inculcated on the lowest class of people', insisted the *Gentleman's Magazine* in the 1790s,[5] and the Charity and Sunday Schools responded with endless variations on the theme of 'the Devil finds employment for idle hands'. The children's hymns urged the virtues of industry:[6]

> *How doth the busy little bee*
> *Improve each shining hour*
> *And gather honey all the day*
> *From every opening flower.*

1. *The substance of two addresses on laying the foundation stone of the Stockport Sunday School* (Stockport, 1805).

2. Beilby Porteus, *A letter to the clergy of the diocese of Chester concerning Sunday Schools* (1786, p. 11).

3. William Brooke, *Short addresses to the children of Sunday Schools* (7th edn., 1811, p. 78).

4. Annual Report of the Stockport Sunday School (Stockport, 1814).

5. Vol. LXVII, 1797, p. 820.

6. Isaac Watts, *Divine and moral songs for children* (1869 edn., p. 38).

In works of labour or of skill
I would be busy too;
For Satan finds some mischief still
For idle hands to do.

In its prayers, too, the child was taught to ask God to 'grant me industry'.[1] The awful consequences of wilful idleness were brought home to the children through the medium of their reading exercises. Let me quote just a single example from Sarah Trimmer's 'Lessons consisting of words not exceeding two syllables' in her *Charity School Spelling Book*: 'John Knight was in the army. He carried a knapsack, and he was no better than a knave, for he did not enlist from a wish to serve his King and Country, but because he did not like work. After doing many bad things he went off, for which he was whipped; after a while he went off again, and then he was shot.'[2]

There may have been other aims of a more generally philanthropic nature, but the priority that the organizers of Charity and Sunday Schools themselves gave to these very particular social aims, and the frequency with which they reasserted them, indicate the degree of importance they attached to them. The scope of this paper does not permit me to illustrate the educational methods by which these aims were translated into action in the classroom. And the question of the extent to which the necessary attitudes were successfully instilled into the rising generations of industrial workers is, in one sense, irrelevant.[3] We are dealing with an Industrial Revolution which is a fact of history: a suitable labour force patently *was* created to man such industrial growth as in fact occurred.[4]

1. White Kennet (Bishop of Peterborough), *The Christian scholar* (1811, p. 46).
2. Mrs Trimmer, *The Charity School spelling book*, Part II (new edn., n.d., p. 24).
3. Twentieth-century studies show a positive, if small, correlation between teachers' and children's attitudes and opinions. There is, of course, a much more significant correlation between parents' and children's opinions. But the eighteenth-century environment differed so markedly from that of the twentieth century that it is difficult to decide whether the correlation between, say, teachers' and children's opinions might have been greater or less in the former period than in the latter (see Fleming, 1959, pp. 42–3).
4. Since this paper was written, a brilliant study of the relationship between education and social and economic change has been published

It is to the third broad group of social theories – that concerned with the quantity and quality of entrepreneurs and innovators – that I wish to devote my principal attention in this paper. These theories study changes in the supply of innovational leadership through shifts in the structure of personality. Two contrasting approaches in this field have been applied to the study of economic development, one by a student of motivational analysis, David C. McClelland (1961), and the other by Everett E. Hagen (1962). Since the latter is dealing elsewhere in this volume with his own theory, I shall confine myself in this paper to the former's historical application of motivational analysis. McClelland's approach sees human action – be it entrepreneurial, technological, or any other sector of action – as resulting from the pursuit of the satisfaction of a range of psychological *needs*, and seeks to understand not so much the direction in which these needs are pursued, as the *intensity* or *drive* with which a chosen direction is followed. Since every personality is unique, individuals will vary in the structure of their need patterns. More important, personality is both inborn and post-natally created. This means that one sector at least of the individual motivational pattern is subject to infantile and childhood (parental and environmental) influences.

There is, it may be imagined, a range of needs, the amalgam of which determines individual motivation. They include the need for affiliation, which is a need for recognition, approval, friendship; the need for knowledge; the need to organize (to restore order out of chaos); and the need for achievement. Of these, it is the last, the need for achievement, that seems to have the most relevance for economic history, since McClelland is able to establish by a wealth of psychometric techniques that a high need for achievement is closely correlated with the principal 'entrepreneurial' personality characteristics, such as special attitudes towards risk-taking,

---

(Dore, *Education in Tokugawa Japan* (1965), particularly Chapter X). Professor Dore's analysis leaves little doubt that educational changes played a significant part in paving the way for Japan's 'take-off'. The pattern of social structure and social mobility in Tokugawa Japan was, of course, very different from that in eighteenth-century Britain, so that the details of the interrelationship between educational policy and the social, economic, and political changes of the 1860s in Japan differ markedly from the British eighteenth-century experience; but the two widely disparate historical backgrounds have clearly many interesting features in common.

willingness to expend energy, willingness to innovate, and a readiness to make decisions and accept responsibility. What is involved in the need for achievement is the need not so much to reach certain goals, such as wealth, status, respect, etc., as to enjoy the satisfaction of success. It has been defined by Murray, who first explored it comprehensively in 1938, as the need 'to accomplish something difficult . . ., to overcome obstacles and attain a high standard . . ., to rival and surpass others . . ., to increase self-regard by the successful exercise of talent' (Murray *et al.*, 1938). McClelland demonstrates that there are wide variations in the strength of the need for achievement not merely between different societies, but also between different time-periods of the same society, and between different individuals or groups of individuals in a single society at a given point in time.

McClelland devised means of measuring the need for achievement in the past, and established an index of variations in its level over the course of British history from the fifteenth century to the early nineteenth century by which he claimed to show that major changes in the pace and direction of economic growth were anticipated at a distance of a generation or so by similar changes in the level of the need for achievement. His index, for example, takes a clear and decisive upturn at the beginning of the eighteenth century – at the moment in time, that is to say, most nicely calculated to prepare the ground for a major spurt in economic growth in the second half of the century. It only remained for him to explain how such a major shift in the general societal level of need for achievement was induced.

Personality, it is argued, is largely, though not wholly, determined in infancy and childhood, and the influences that operate most effectively on the level of need for achievement seem to be those that are brought to bear on children between the ages of four and ten. There are wide variations between different cultural, social, and religious backgrounds in the attitudes of parents to child-rearing, and the condition that McClelland found was optimal for maximizing need for achievement was one of conscious training for self-reliance and mastery which kept clear of the extremes of leaving the child to make its own way (arising from sheer neglect or indifference), on the one hand, and of excessive restrictiveness and authoritarianism, on the other. McClelland takes the view that the single most powerful influence on the level of need for achievement is the religious background, and I would suggest that, by isolating with some precision just what factors in the home, be it a Protestant, a Catholic, a Buddhist, or a Hindu home, are relevant to the level of entrepreneurial and innovational activity, McClelland has brought a new and valuable precision to the old problem of 'religion and the rise of capitalism'. He is not prepared, on the basis of mere apparent logic, to equate a Protestant reformation with a surge of economic activity, arguing that Lutheranism, for example, 'was in many respects more authoritarian than Roman Catholicism', and relating this to his finding that an authoritarian environment tended not to maximize the need for achievement. Nevertheless, by means of a long series of correlative studies into variations in childhood influences in Protestant, Jewish, French-Canadian Catholic, Italian Catholic, and many other national-religious backgrounds, he concluded that individualistic religions tend, in broad terms, to be associated with high need for achievement, in contrast to authoritarian religions, which are commonly associated with lower levels of need for achievement. In particular, 'the more traditional Catholics do appear to have some of the values and attitudes that would be associated with lower need for achievement', while Protestants tend to 'favour earlier independence and mastery training than do various Catholic groups', though he conceded that there are nowadays, at least, wide variations and subcultures among Catholic communities.

McClelland's case is far more intricate and elaborate than I have been able to indicate in such a brief summary of his thesis. Nevertheless, as he himself admits (1961, p. 61), 'there is some flaw in nearly every finding reported – some alternative explanation of the result obtained'. It requires a psychologist and not a historian to assess the validity of McClelland's techniques and statistical findings, and it is worth noting that at least one fellow-psychologist has expressed some scepticism over inferences drawn from the particular statistical methods adopted by McClelland. Nonetheless, the same reviewer accepts this claim that 'achievement motivation is an important factor affecting the rate of economic development' (Smith, 1964, p. 372).

While McClelland's approach is theoretical in the sense that he has sought a method of analysis which is *generally* applicable to any situation of acceleration or deceleration of economic growth, my concern in this paper is with only one such situation, and I am interested therefore in assessing the usefulness of his theory solely in the context of the British Industrial Revolution of the eighteenth century. One virtue of any theory is that it prompts the asking of a range of questions, and this theory asks some very specific questions about British society before the Industrial Revolution. What, first, were the precise chronologies of the growth of the Protestant dissenting sects? How did these chronologies relate to the chronology of economic growth? Did the sects in fact produce a disproportionate share of the increased flow of entrepreneurs and inventors in the eighteenth century? Did these sects foster child-rearing practices that differed in any significant ways from those of the established church, or from those common in the period before their emergence?

In spite of the vast outpouring of words in the 'religion and the rise of capitalism' debate, few of the participants have gone to much trouble to assess the changes in the actual or proportional strength of the various dissenting sects in England over the whole period before and during the Industrial Revolution. Since the relative strength of the sects is fundamental to all discussion linking religious with economic changes, it is worth digressing briefly in order to consider this problem. A number of contemporary estimates of dissenting congregations were made in this period, and although they obviously cannot pretend to complete accuracy, they were made by knowledgeable dissenting ministers who were dealing with a field limited enough in size to be within the scope of a single investigator.

The expression 'dissenting congregation' has no significant reality in English history until the Restoration of 1660, when some 2,000 ministers were ejected from their livings on account of their refusal to accept the restored Anglican authority. If these ministers took their congregations with them, the intense persecution that occupied the next dozen years whittled their numbers down to little more than half; and the indications are that there was little actual growth (and therefore – in view of the rising population – some relative decline) in the number of dissenting congregations until at least 1775 and possibly even later. There was, it has been estimated, an actual decline in dissenting congregations in London from sixty to fifty-eight between 1695 and 1730. The decisive growth in numbers occurred after 1775. Daniel Neal estimated there to have been 1,150 dissenting congregations in 1715/16; Josiah Thompson's estimate for 1772 put the figure at 1,254, a figure we can set beside Robert Robinson's estimate of 1,118 for England alone for 1775 (the Welsh counties in Robinson's estimate accounting almost exactly for the difference). By 1812, according to Bogue and Bennett, the figure had just topped 2,000. All these estimates break down the totals by counties, and the extremely close similarity of the very varied county strengths in Thompson's and Robinson's figures for 1772 and 1775 respectively is reassuring. Robinson also supplied a detailed analysis of his own county of Cambridgeshire, which showed an average church membership of 140 for twenty-one congregations. Since church membership at this time probably included all over the age of about twelve or fourteen, something of the order of 40 per cent ought probably to be added to allow for children and for comparison with the total population. On this reckoning, dissenters are unlikely to have numbered much more than a quarter of a million in the 1770s, when the population of England and Wales must have been in the region of seven and a half million – 3 per cent only of the total. On the same basis, the proportion is not likely to have risen to more than 5 per cent by 1812.[1]

However, dissenters, according to all these estimates, included only the Presbyterian, Congregational, and Baptist churches. What about Quakers and Unitarians who played an all-important part in the eighteenth-century economy? I have not found any numerical assessment of the strength of Quakerism in this period, but, if only to offer something firm, I shall venture two generalizations: first, that Quakers were never more than a very small minority indeed; and, second, that their numerical strength declined relatively, and, possibly, actually, during the eighteenth century. One per cent of the total population in, say, 1775, would have given them upwards of 75,000, and I doubt if they commanded even this following then. The Unitarians mostly hived off the Congregationalists during the second half of the eighteenth century and did not therefore add noticeably to the total number of dissenters (see

1. The estimates for 1715/16, 1772, and 1820 are given in D. Bogue and J. Bennett, *History of dissenters*, Vol. II (1809, pp. 98–9); Vol. III (1810, p. 330); and Vol. IV (1812, pp. 327–8). Robinson's figures for 1775 are given in George Dyer, *Memoirs of the life and writings of Robert Robinson* (1796, pp. 461–3).

Griffiths, 1935). They were almost certainly the smallest of all these groups, though they combined in a most significant way the maximum degree of freedom of thought with maximum persecution.

One other trend of some interest is revealed by these estimates – a marked shift in the relative positions of the Presbyterian and Congregational churches: whereas in 1715/16 there were 750 Presbyterian and 150 Congregational (Independent) congregations in England and Wales out of 1,150, by 1820 there were 1,024 Congregational and only 270 Presbyterian congregations out of 2,000. This relative growth of Congregationalism is of some note in view of some findings I shall report below.

In all this I have made no mention of Methodism. Though Methodism did not really enjoy any separate existence from the Church of England until 1784, as a way of life it undoubtedly began to exercise its influence from the 1740s. And though no figures, unfortunately, are available, there is little doubt that its followers were numerous – probably far more numerous than the dissenting sects – by the 1780s. Thus, although the principal social significance of Methodism undoubtedly lies in the field of consequences rather than of causes of the Industrial Revolution (and therefore falls outside my province), there may well have been a relatively numerous generation brought up under Methodist influence arriving at adulthood at the time of the take-off.

The lessons of this digression into ecclesiastical history are, I suggest, as follows: first, that the substantial growth of dissent was a feature of the actual period of the Industrial Revolution, and that, before it, dissenters really were a very small minority. Even if the Methodists are taken into account, Samuelsson's (1962, p. 125), assertion 'that roughly half the inhabitants of England belonged to nonconformist denominations at the time of the Industrial Revolution' simply cannot be accepted. The second point is the growing strength of Congregationalism, and with it (because deriving from it) Unitarianism, to a dominant position in English dissent by the end of the eighteenth century.

So far as the proportion of nonconformist entrepreneurs and inventors is concerned, we have as a starting-point Hagen's admirable analysis of ninety-two leading entrepreneurs of the British Industrial Revolution. These ninety-two were, of course, only a minority of all the entrepreneurs and inventors of the period, and it is not impossible that the majority, of whose history and religious affiliations we remain largely ignorant, did not conform exactly to the pattern of church membership established by Hagen for his ninety-two specimens. Nonetheless, the 41 per cent of the English, or 49 per cent of the British, he showed as nonconformists is unlikely to be wildly misleading: a final analysis might turn out to be somewhat divergent, but must be sufficiently far from the minute estimates of dissenting strength to leave a very significant disparity to be explained (Hagen, 1962, pp. 305–8). Thus, though I would accept that there is an important area of doubt still surrounding this particular point, I propose for the purposes of this paper (in common with most historians of the Industrial Revolution) to take a substantial disparity between the proportion of nonconformists in society and the proportion who were successful entrepreneurs as an assumption basic to my further argument.

We now come to the question of whether the dissenting sects tended to indulge in child-rearing practices that differed significantly from those common at the time, or common in the Anglican majority of the population, and whether these child-rearing practices, if they did so differ, would have tended to induce a different level of the need for achievement. This is a particularly elusive aspect of history, and while my own idleness may explain in part an unimpressive documentation of this part of my paper, the sheer difficulty of finding out just how parents in different sections of the community treated their children 250 years ago also plays a part in this shortcoming. There is, for example, an extremely interesting assertion made by Isaac Watts in the 1720s, to the effect that there had been some important shifts in general attitudes to child-rearing in England in the century or so before he wrote. 'In the beginning of the last century [the seventeenth century],' he wrote, 'and so onward to the middle of it, the children were usually obliged to believe what their parents and their masters taught them, whether they were principles of science, or articles of faith and practice: they were tied down almost to every punctilio, as though it were necessary to salvation.' 'But in this [the eighteenth] century', he went on to say, 'when the doctrine of a just and reasonable liberty is better known, too many of the present youth break all the bonds of nature and duty, and run to the wildest degrees of looseness, both in belief and practice. ... The son nowadays forgets the obligations he is under to honour and obey the persons

c

that gave him birth.... So wanton and licentious a spirit has possessed some of the youth of the nation, that they never think they have freed themselves from the prejudices of their education till they have thrown off almost all the yokes of restraint that are laid upon them by God or man.'[1] Confirmation of this switch, from the extremes of authoritarianism on the one hand to those of libertarianism on the other, would be extremely valuable, but is not so far forthcoming. The tendency of child-rearing practices of either of these kinds would be, according to McClelland, not to maximize the need for achievement, and, by setting a general societal level somewhere below the maximum, to leave room for some raising of the level of need for achievement as a result of innovations in child-rearing practices in either the late seventeenth or the eighteenth century.

McClelland's index of need for achievement in Britain takes a strongly upward turn at the beginning of the eighteenth century. McClelland himself explains this upturn in terms of the Methodist revival, saying that the Methodists' 'uncompromising stress on excellence seems almost certain to have acted to promote the development of achievement motivation in Methodist children' (1961, p. 146). The scope of McClelland's work evidently prevented him from examining this mechanism very closely, and in what follows I shall try to fill the gap.

Let me repeat the conditions which, according to McClelland, tend to maximize need for achievement: 'Early mastery training', he says (1961, p. 345), 'promotes high need for achievement, *provided* it does not reflect generalized restrictiveness, authoritarianism, or "rejection" by the parents.' The Methodist revival did, indeed, introduce an interesting new approach. For the Methodists the Bible was, above all, the guide, in a most literal sense, to action. So far as child-rearing was concerned, the Methodists preferred to pass quickly by the softer injunctions of the word of Jesus himself in the New Testament, and to seek guidance in the harsher world of the Old Testament – in the book of Proverbs. And the book of Proverbs is quite unequivocal in this respect: 'Foolishness is bound up in the heart of a child, but the rod of correction shall drive it from him.' 'Withhold not correction from a child; for if thou beat him with the rod he shall not die: thou shalt beat him with the rod and shall deliver his soul from hell.' 'Correct thy son

1. Isaac Watts, *Works*, Vol. V (1810, pp. 393–4).

while there is hope, and let not thy soul spare for his crying.' 'He
that spareth the rod, hateth his son; but he that loveth him,
chasteneth him betimes.'[1] These, and many similar approving
references to the 'rod of correction', were quoted endlessly and
enthusiastically by the Methodists. But while Doddridge, the
Congregationalist, who also quoted some of them, went on to
recommend moderation of severity,[2] for Welsey himself the book of
Proverbs was even 'soft' on children. The doctrine of original sin
dominated his approach to child-rearing: in seeking to suppress the
evil already implanted in a babe at birth, Wesley's educational
theory was wholly negative, in sharp contrast to the positive
approach of the Congregationalists and early Quakers. Child-
rearing, for Wesley, was a medical process of curing what he called
the diseases of a child's nature. These diseases were atheism, the
child's own will, pride, love of the world, anger, deviation from
truth, or speaking or acting contrary to justice. It is apparent from
his own emphasis that only one of these diseases really mattered –
self-will; and his whole approach to the bringing-up of children
was concentrated on the destruction of a child's will. 'In the whole
art of Christian education', he said, 'there is nothing more important than this.' 'The wise parent,' he advocated, therefore, 'should
begin to break their will the first moment it appears. Whatever
pain it cost, conquer their stubbornness; break the will, if you
would not damn the child. I conjure you not to neglect, not to
delay this! Therefore, (1) Let a child from a year old be taught to
fear the rod and to cry softly. In order to do this; (2) Let him have
nothing he cries for; absolutely nothing, great or small; else you
undo your own work. (3) At all events, from that age, make him
do as he is bid, if you whip him ten times running to effect it.
Let none persuade you it is cruelty to do this, it is cruelty not to
do it. Break his will now, and his soul will live, and he will probably
bless you to all eternity.' 'Do not "spare the rod and spoil the
child": if you have not the heart of a tiger, do not give your child
up to his own will, that is, to the devil. . . . Make them submit,
that they may not perish. Break their wills that you may save their
soul.'[3]

1. *Proverbs*, xxii, 15; xxiii, 13, 14; xix, 18; xiii, 24.
2. Philip Doddridge, *Works*, Vol. II (1803, p. 49). Leeds.
3. John Wesley, *Sermons on several occasions*, Vol. II (1825, pp. 493–
7).

In requiring parents to 'teach your children, as soon as possibly you can, that they are fallen spirits . . ., that in foolish desires and grovelling appetites they are like beasts of the field',[1] Wesley was insisting on conditions of child-rearing that were unlikely to maximize the need for achievement. Conceivably, Methodist parents did not always achieve the full rigour of the Wesleyan régime, but the general tendency of Methodism and Methodist attitudes to child-rearing must nevertheless have been away from conditions likely to maximize the need for achievement. It is thus, possibly, no coincidence that Hagen's list of ninety-two successful entrepreneurs of the Industrial Revolution includes only two known Methodists, though Methodists were certainly likely to have had a following of more than 2 per cent of the population by the early nineteenth century. The effect of this reasoning, for what it is worth, coupled with the relative lateness of arrival on the economic scene of Methodism, would be to suggest that the likelihood of Methodism's having contributed in social ways to the origins of the Industrial Revolution is slight.

Thus, using McClelland's own criteria, I would suggest that his correlation between rising need for achievement and the Methodist revival is questionable. I think McClelland probably made the correlation because of the coincidence in timing, and because of the Methodists' 'drive for excellence'. But he might have noticed that his index of need for achievement started to rise forty years before Methodism effectively appeared on the scene, and it was unfortunate not to have appreciated that the Methodist ideals in child-rearing fitted only some and not all of his conditions for maximizing the need for achievement.

Is there any possibility that the other nonconformist sects fit his conditions more fully in this period? So far as the Quakers were concerned, Braithwaite, their historian, believes that two phases may be distinguished. The first generation of Quakers, fighting for their beliefs in the face of fierce persecution, insisted above all on a freedom of individual thought and choice which they passed down to their own children tempered by their characteristic care for their outward behaviour and social attitudes. As another historian of the Society of Friends has expressed it: 'Their break with the rites and dogmas of the historical churches as well as with many social customs and political ties gave them original and fresh

1. Ibid, pp. 498–9.

viewpoints and encouraged educational pioneering and adventure' (Russell, 1942, p. 155). Penn's ideas on education, for example, display an abhorrence of stultifying rote-learning and a desire to stimulate a child's intellectual processes and natural curiosity. 'Be sure to observe their [the children's] genius, and do not cross it as to learning', he wrote.[1] But the coming of *de facto* toleration towards the end of the seventeenth century produced in the second generation of Quakers, according to Braithwaite (1919, p. 537), a hardening of attitudes, an ebbing of liberality – in his own words, 'a sterilizing leadership of authority'. The practice of sending the children of Quakers to boarding-schools became more common, and the stress in Quaker attitudes to the upbringing of children shifted towards belief in 'the efficacy of outward regulation'. 'There is no vision', says Braithwaite (p. 536) of this period, 'of the higher meaning of true education as we understand it today.'

If this distinction is a valid one, then it may mean that the influences brought to bear on Quaker children brought up before 1700 were slightly more inclined, on balance, to maximize need for achievement than were those bearing on children brought up by Quakers in the eighteenth century, and this may possibly help to explain why the period of Quaker dominance in English industry tends to be early rather than late in the eighteenth century. Is there any significance in the fact that Abraham Darby, Ambrose Crowley, Charles Lloyd, and William Rawlinson, to mention but a few of the great entrepreneurs with Quaker backgrounds, were brought up in the first, less authoritarian phase of the Society of Friends?

The Congregational Isaac Watts posed the question, 'Is there no medium between these two extremes – excess of confinement and excess of liberty?', and answered it, 'Yes, surely; there have been happy instances . . . both of parents and children that have learned to tread this middle path'.[2] The Congregationalists, the most vigorous of the dissenting sects in the eighteenth century, from whom the Unitarians sprang, appear to have nurtured a conception of child-rearing most closely related to the conditions which, according to McClelland, were most likely to maximize the need for achievement. William Belsham, for example, who spoke of 'that mild wisdom which secures the affections while it

1. In a letter of 1682, quoted by W. C. Braithwaite (1919, p. 529).
2. Isaac Watts, *Works*, Vol. V (1810, p. 395).

informs the understanding', also insisted 'that the culture of the
human mind cannot commence at too early a period'. And while,
on the one hand, he referred with the utmost scorn to Rousseau's
idea of 'keeping children in ignorance till they have attained an
age in which they can judge without prejudice', he objected equally
strongly to the opposite authoritarian extreme 'that the parental
authority ought to be exercised with rigour, and that implicit
obedience is almost the only lesson which needs to be inculcated'.[1]
His preference for a middle path, which encouraged the child to
learn under a parental régime that kept clear of the extremes of
authoritarianism and neglect, had already been advocated by
Philip Doddridge. 'I would by no means drive matters to extremi-
ties', Doddridge advised, speaking of parental discipline. 'Take
heed that your corrections be not too frequent or too severe. . . .
If your correction be too frequent, it will probably spoil much of
the success. Your children, like iron, will harden under repeated
strokes.'[2]

Quite the most comprehensive outline of ideal child-rearing
practices came from Isaac Watts. In answer to the question, 'Is it
not possible for the parent to indulge, and the child to enjoy, a
just liberty, and yet neither encourage nor practise a wild licen-
tiousness?', he gave an account of the upbringing of an imaginary
youth, Eugenio. This paragon of virtue, energy, imagination,
ability, and, we may be sure, need for achievement, was brought
up on lines which McClelland himself could hardly have bettered!
'He was trained up from the very cradle to all the duties of infant
virtue by the allurements of love and reward, suited to his age;
and never was driven to practise anything by a frown or hasty
word, where it was possible for tender affections to work the same
effect by indulgence and delay. . . . As fast as his reasoning powers
began to appear and exert themselves, they were conducted in any
easy track of thought, to find out and observe the reasonableness
of every part of his duty. . . . He was enticed sometimes to a love of
letters, by making his lesson a reward of some domestic duty; and
a permission to pursue some parts of learning was the appointed
recompense of his diligence and improvement in others.'[3]

1. W. Belsham, *Essays philosophical and moral, historical and literary*,
Vol. I (1799, pp. 397, 399).
2. Philip Doddridge, *Works*, Vol. II (1803, p. 49). Leeds.
3. Isaac Watts, *Works*, Vol. V (1810, pp. 395–6).

One can hardly avoid noticing that, while the same theme of obedience runs through much of contemporary thought in relation to the education of all social classes, there is a sharp contrast between the humane tone of the dissenting approach to middle-class education and the utilitarian asperity of the requirements of all parties for working-class education. The dichotomy is most sharply expressed in the writings of Isaac Watts. Like many of his contemporaries, Watts employed a dual set of standards – one for the education of the labouring classes, and another for the middle class. And since both a class of entrepreneurs and a proletariat, with sharply contrasting social attitudes, were essential prerequisites of rapid industrialization, it may be that the dual standards of Isaac Watts were most finely calculated to achieve growth. That such dual standards existed seems to me beyond doubt: whether they played a significant role in the acceleration of the rate of growth must, in the nature of this type of historical evidence, remain, for the time being at least, a matter of opinion. It is important to stress, however, that rapid economic growth was *not* the goal of this type of child-rearing and educational dualism. This result (assuming the child-rearing practices to have had some bearing on the rate of economic growth) was quite unintentional. To adapt Adam Smith slightly from a not unrelated context: 'They intend only their own gain, and they are in this, as in many other cases, led by an invisible hand to promote an end which was no part of their intention.' The economic historian, of course, is more concerned with the result than with the intention.

While it might be desirable, for the purposes of analysis of non-economic factors in growth, to relegate the economic factors to the role of parameters, it is, nevertheless, important to let the natural balance between both sets of factors reassert itself. In the analysis of the take-off, the quest for a *cause unique* is as fatal as it is alluring: to insist on a single prime mover involves denial of the roles of expanding demand both at home and overseas, of an abundance of capital, and of changes in the rate of growth of population springing from non-economic origins. The social and cultural changes must, I am sure, drop into place beside their economic companions. Economic development is a complex process, and, if it may be necessary on occasion to isolate a single aspect of growth, as I have done in this paper, it is all the more important to ensure that perspectives are finally restored.

Accepting this complexity of the growth process, most economists and economic historians are, I imagine, prepared to allocate some role to non-economic factors; but there is a wide range of attitudes to them. Those with wide experience of the struggles of underdeveloped countries in the world today to get off the ground tend, empirically, to rate the non-economic variables pretty highly; those, on the other hand, concerned more theoretically with models of growth embodying a fair degree of mathematical precision tend to take no account of the non-economic elements, not because they do not acknowledge their existence, but because there can, at this early stage, be no measurement of this category of factor. Nonetheless, the non-economic factors continue stubbornly and vigorously to assert their existence. McClelland's (1961, p. 391) claim that 'the whole view of history shifts once the importance of the achievement motive is recognized' may be an exaggeration, but it cannot be wholly wrong. Social theory has opened some doors which are adding a valuable and exciting new dimension not merely to the study of the Industrial Revolution, but also to the analysis of economic development generally. The historian of the Industrial Revolution may flounder in the pursuit of the answer to new kinds of questions; he will certainly never succeed entirely; the nature of historical evidence is almost always such that absolute certainty is beyond his grasp. But is it not possible that psychometry has now advanced sufficiently far to have become a likely ally to the sociologist and the economist? – that the study of personality has passed beyond the stage of what Gerschenkron (1965) recently called 'mere speculation about things that are unknown and in all likelihood unknowable'? I would venture to suggest, in conclusion, that the kinds of interdisciplinary study that create almost insuperable problems for the historian on account of the elusiveness of the appropriate evidence may even now, thanks to advances in the ability of psychologists to quantify, be a practical proposition for students of current economic development.

REFERENCES

AITKEN, H. G. J. (ed.) (1965) *Explorations in enterprise.* Cambridge, Mass.: Harvard University Press.

ASHTON, T. S. (1948) *The industrial revolution, 1760–1830.* London: Oxford University Press.

BRAITHWAITE, W. C. (1919) *The second period of Quakerism.* London: Cambridge University Press.

COCHRAN, T. C. (1949) Role and sanction in American entrepreneurial history. In *Change and the entrepreneur.* Research Center in Entrepreneurial History, Harvard University. Cambridge, Mass.: Harvard University Press. (Reprinted in H. G. J. Aitken (ed.), *Explorations in enterprise,* 1965, pp. 93–112.)

DOMAR, E. D. (1957) *Essays in the theory of economic growth.* New York: Oxford University Press.

DORE, R. P. (1965) *Education in Tokugawa Japan.* Berkeley: University of California Press; London: Routledge & Kegan Paul.

FLEMING, C. M. (1959) *The social psychology of education.* (2nd rev. edn.) London: Routledge & Kegan Paul.

GRIFFITHS, O. M. (1935) *Religion and learning.* London: Cambridge University Press.

GERSCHENKRON, A. (1965) Review of E. E. Hagen, *On the theory of social change,* in *Economica,* n.s. xxxii, p. 94.

HAGEN, E. E. (1962) *On the theory of social change.* Homewood, Ill.: Dorsey Press; London: Tavistock Publications, 1964.

HOSELITZ, B. F. (1960) *Sociological aspects of economic growth.* Glencoe, Ill.: Free Press; London: Collier-Macmillan.

LINTON, R. (1936) *The study of man: an introduction.* New York: Appleton-Century.

MCCLELLAND, D. C. (1961) *The achieving society.* Princeton, N.J.: Van Nostrand.

MURRAY, H. A. *et al.* (1938) *Explorations in personality.* New York: Oxford University Press.

PARSONS, T. (1951) *The social system.* Glencoe, Ill.: Free Press.

PARSONS, T. & SHILS, E. A. (eds.) (1952) *Toward a general theory of action.* Cambridge, Mass.: Harvard University Press.

ROSTOW, W. W. (1960) *The stages of economic growth.* London: Cambridge University Press.

RUSSELL, E. (1942) *The history of Quakerism.* New York: Macmillan.

SAMUELSSON, K. (1962) *Religion and economic action.* New York: Basic Books.

SMITH, ADAM (1776) *The wealth of nations.* Edited by E. Cannan, London, 1904. Vol. II, pp. 272–3.

SMITH, M. BREWSTER (1964) Review of D. C. McClelland, *The achieving society,* in *History and theory* **3**, 372.

WADSWORTH, A. P. (1950–51). The first Manchester Sunday Schools. *Bulletin of the John Rylands Library,* **33**, 300.

WETHERELL, PHYLLIS J. (1950) Education and the children's hymn in eighteenth-century England. In S. C. McCulloch (ed.), *British humanitarianism: essays honoring Frank J. Klingberg.* Philadelphia: Church Hist. Soc.

British Personality
and the Industrial Revolution:
The Historical Evidence

EVERETT E. HAGEN

Some readers of a book of mine, *On the Theory of Social Change* (1962), have drawn from it the conclusion that I believe that there can be no increase in innovational activity in a society without change in personality between generations, resulting from change in childhood environment. In that book I do not summarize my argument, but rather let it develop in a somewhat complex way. Because of this, and because of the stress I place on personality change as a neglected element in historical explanation, to draw that conclusion is reasonable. I should like, therefore, to note at the beginning of this paper that it is incorrect. I do not believe, and did not believe when I wrote that volume, that personality change is the only possible or important cause of an increase in innovational activity.

In many historical cases of an increase in the level of innovational activity by a social group, the best explanation seems to be that the group was faced with a new problem in circumstances in which its old pattern of response was not possible. Examples of circumstances which have produced these results are the colonization of 'empty lands', such as those of North America, Australia, and New Zealand, and drastic disruption of the social order by war. During the Second World War, the people of Germany, Japan, France, and Italy received severe psychological shocks. The social order proved impotent. Probably the people of these countries were, so to speak, jolted out of old psychological and social ruts. Especially in Germany and Japan, extensive physical destruction also occurred, so that producers could not continue in old technical ruts. Surely these shocks are plausible partial explanations of the sharp increase in the rate of technical innovation in Germany, France, Italy, and Japan since the war. In these instances, no doubt there were also personality changes from one generation to the next, and perhaps within the same generation, for severe social traumata may change men's emotional mechanisms; but apart from these changes in personality the pace of innovation probably increased simply because, blasted out of old ruts, individuals were forced to struggle towards new solutions.

But one person may also solve problems more successfully than another because he is a better problem-solver. Moreover, the source of this ability is not necessarily that he inherited better mental equipment. Rather, during his early years, his parents and the other persons important to him in his home may have provided a secure and supporting environment for the use of his initiative; may have stimulated and rewarded him when he solved problems; and, when his neuro-muscular development was such that he could do various tasks for himself, may have penalized him by displeasure when he failed to do them. If so, he may have learned confidence and satisfaction in the use of his judgement, may have a firm sense that the world is an orderly place which may be expected to respond satisfactorily to his initiative, and a sense of unease when he depends on someone else for action. Because of these traits, all his life he may be drawn towards opportunities to make improvements by solving difficulties or rearranging the elements in the circumstances around him. He will act upon difficulties not merely to gain an end but because it is fun to do so (or because a sense of unease within him is at least somewhat relieved while he is working at a problem).

Another person, whose early environment was an emotionally undependable or an anxious and confining one, or one that compulsively pressed him to achieve the many difficult learning tasks of infancy and childhood before his neuro-muscular development had reached the necessary stage, may have learned to feel anxiety whenever he faces a problem. If so, he may, throughout his later life, neglect to notice opportunities for change. Thus he avoids anxiety. Or, having discovered a procedure that works well, he may cling compulsively to it even when circumstances have changed and the procedure is no longer appropriate.[1]

Since creativity is greatly influenced by the family environ-

1. Concerning the qualities of personality associated with creativity, see, for example, Anderson (1959).

ment which impinges upon an individual during his early forma-
tive years, and since family environment, methods of child-
training, and later childhood environment may all differ among
societies and from one era to another, it follows that the incidence
of somewhat greater than average creativity may be higher among
one people than among another, in any given historical epoch. The
same may be true of other aspects of personality. Hence differences
among societies with respect to personality may be an important
historical force.

The main thesis of this paper is that differences in personality
rather than differential circumstances are the central explanation
of Britain's primacy in the Industrial Revolution. In my judgement, the Industrial Revolution occurred first in England and
Wales not simply because the circumstances facing Britain were
different from those facing Continental countries but because
British people were inwardly different from those of the Continent.
I shall suggest that between, say, A.D. 1200 and 1800 the British
people solved problems in several fields more successfully than
did their Continental contemporaries, that the most plausible
cause of their greater effectiveness is a difference in personality,
and that the difference in personality that is thus manifested is also
the probable cause of the greater British success in technical
innovation. I shall not speculate here concerning the possible
causes of the difference in personality.[1] I shall merely summarize
the historical facts which suggest to me that it existed.

One consideration in favour of any explanatory hypothesis in any
field is the weakness or incompleteness of the alternatives. It
would therefore be appropriate to consider here the conventional
(mainly economic) explanations of Britain's primacy. However,
though these explanations seem to me to consist mainly of a not
very convincing sort of 'retrospective inference' ('something
must have caused Britain's primacy in time, so presumably the
earlier conditions overtly observable did'), I cannot, within the
scope of the present paper, undertake their criticism. Rather, I
must merely suggest some evidence of differences in personality,

1. I have done so in *On the theory of social change* (1962). It is perhaps
apparent, from the cursory references to personality formation in the text
above, that I believe that the causes must include circumstances which
impinged on the home; that they did not consist merely of concepts
learned in formal education.

and let other scholars make such comparative evaluations as seem justified. Even in presenting the positive evidence, I shall necessarily write in broad sweeps. The sketch below is not a closely reasoned historical argument; to put forward such an argument concerning the complex question under discussion would require a large volume. In this paper, then, I am merely offering a hypothesis for research. But since it is the broad trends in a society's development with which one would expect the personality characteristics of the members of the society to be associated, painting with a broad brush is not entirely inappropriate.

The evidence, being historical, is necessarily diffuse. With regard to any explanation in history except the proximate cause of a specific event, that is the only sort of evidence there is, and hence is the sort one must put up with.

Before the eighteenth century, Britain was technically behind one or another Continental country in almost all fields. By the seventeenth century, she had caught up with the Dutch and Flemish in spinning and in most kinds of weaving, but the Flemish were still ahead in dyeing and finishing and in some specialized weaving. The Dutch were pre-eminent before the eighteenth century in many crafts: printing and type-founding, glass-making, etc. They were the world's leaders in the carrying trade. They were the world's best merchant shipbuilders. (So surprising is this fact to some observers that it is worth repeating that even at the end of the seventeenth century the British were not the best shipbuilders. They were still copying technical advances developed on the Continent.) The Dutch were the world's leaders in the management of government finance, in financial organization, and in business management. By 1625 the Amsterdam exchanges were greatly facilitating trade and capital transactions by quoting uniform prices for more than three hundred commodities, and for the shares of Dutch trading companies. And in 1690, in an English–Dutch campaign in Ireland against an opposing coalition, a Dutch firm was hired to supply the English–Dutch army. There seems to have been no British firm capable of managing the logistics involved.

In the sixteenth century, the Germans were ahead of the British in almost all branches of mining and metallurgy, and apparently (though this is not clear) they maintained their superiority in a number of fields in the seventeenth. In the seventeenth century, better iron-casting was done on the Continent than in Britain, and, when steel of the best quality was wanted, Britain imported it from Sweden. (The Swedes had a natural resource advantage: their iron ore was more free of sulphur; but their metallurgy was also extremely good.) Apart from clocks, Germany led Britain in the making of precision instruments until the last quarter of the seventeenth century.

However, for several centuries Britain had been catching up. Her faster pace of advance is noticeable from at least the fifteenth century. In the sixteenth century, under Hawkins's brilliant leadership, she evolved the world's best naval organization. In the sixteenth century also, and a little earlier in the century than the Dutch, she devised joint stock companies and thus greatly increased her ability to carry on risky trading and colonizing ventures. In the thirteenth and fourteenth centuries, Britain reared sheep and exported raw wool, mainly to the Flemish. She could not compete in its processing. In the fifteenth century, however, English craftsmen became able to spin and weave as efficiently as those on the Continent, and England began to export grey goods. In the sixteenth and seventeenth centuries, a goodly share of the technical innovations in spinning and weaving occurred first in England – perhaps not a larger number than on the Continent as a whole, but certainly more than in any other one country.[1] In the seventeenth century, Britain overtook the Flemish in the dyeing and finishing of wool and other textiles.

In this century also, having seen the advantages, for a variety of purposes, of the cotton goods produced in India, England made the technical changes necessary for cotton-weaving far sooner than did her Continental rivals. She gained almost a world monopoly in the industry, not because her fleet prevented other countries from exporting (it did not), but because England began to make an unrivalled product. There seems to be some basis for the Indian claim that, when the East India Company forced its way into India, India was the world's best producer of cotton textiles, and that to provide a market for their goods in India the British suppressed the Indian industry by force. However, Britain's great and

---

1. This is a broad statement concerning a complex matter. Many advances seem to have taken place in two or more countries at about the same time. When this was true, England seems usually to have been one of the two. The general statement in the text above seems justified.

long-continuing world advantage in the cotton textile industry did not result merely from her alertness in seeing the good qualities of the cotton textiles of India, but because of her technical advances. When Britain had been behind the Continental countries technically in the wool textile industry, she advanced upon them and surpassed them, because of her continuing more effective innovation. However, when the Continental countries perceived the advantages of Britain's new cotton textile industry, they were unable to catch up with her, because they were first too sluggish in turning to the new industry and then insufficiently innovational to overcome the British lead. On the contrary, that lead widened from the introduction of the weaving of all-cotton textiles in England in the seventeenth century throughout the eighteenth century.

While Britain's industries in general were advancing in the seventeenth century relative to those of other countries, her iron industry was not. During the last half of the century, many forges were closed, because they could not compete with the Continental producers. Output expanded slowly again in the eighteenth century, but Ashton (1951, pp. 20–21 and 60) accepts the estimate that between 1700 and 1775 it increased by not more than 1 per cent per year (while output elsewhere was increasing at a much faster rate). British ironmasters attributed their absolute decline in the last half of the seventeenth century and their relative decline in the eighteenth to the superior advantages (presumably in iron ore and coal deposits) and lower wages of the Continental industry. But with this exception the relative industrial growth was widespread, as is evidenced by the fact that in 1660 Britain produced five times the coal production of the other countries of the world combined.[1]

The great advances of the eighteenth century are too well known to need listing here. But it is pertinent to mention one aspect of Britain's eighteenth-century technical achievements that is not sufficiently stressed in some accounts, namely, their diversity. Important though the steam engine was, the Industrial Revolution was not the result merely of a few great inventions and their

1. Singer, Holmyard, Hall, and Williams (1957, p. 77). The summary account of technical trends in Western Europe from the fifteenth to the eighteenth century is taken mainly from this volume, and also from Clapham (1949).

corollaries. Rather, there were varied advances in many fields: textiles; iron and steel; chemistry (it was perhaps too early to speak of chemical engineering); power; coal-mining; the construction of canals, roads, and bridges; civil engineering; mechanical engineering; botany, agronomy, and many other aspects of agriculture; business organization and management; and, above all, a phenomenon not fully included in any or all of these fields, the invention of a great variety of new machines and productive processes. A gradually swelling stream widened and deepened into a great rushing river. But the change was not nearly as abrupt as accounts that take the mid-eighteenth century as their starting-point sometimes imply. What occurred was an acceleration of a process that had long been going on.

So blasé have we become about modern technical progress that we tend to think of the advances of the eighteenth century as the natural result, given sufficient economic incentive, of the cumulating progress of physical knowledge. They were not. They were the products of technical ingenuity far more than of scientific logic. There is no connexion between the law of universal gravitation or the three laws of motion and the fly shuttle, the steam engine, or Cort's puddling and rolling process of purifying steel – except that they all manifest an unusual degree of creativity.

Of the four great Asian nations, Japan possesses the poorest natural resources, and during the seventeenth, eighteenth, and nineteenth centuries had both the least investment from the West and the least contact with the West. Yet Japan led the others in industrialization. It is difficult to account for that fact except by saying, 'The Japanese are different'. Once one accepts within the framework of one's thinking the concept of differences among societies with respect to personality, such a difference in personality also becomes one plausible explanation of the diverse and long-continued superiority of Britain in technical innovation during the early modern era and the eighteenth century.

Among the relevant evidence of a difference in personality between the British people and those of the Western Continental countries, during the several centuries before the Industrial Revolution, is the comparative behaviour of the British and the Continental societies in the field of government.

Two characteristics of persons who are innovational in social affairs are pertinent. One, sketched briefly above, is trust in one's

D

own capacity, and a resulting willingness to approach the world
around one and operate upon it. Another characteristic of most
innovational persons, which is of especial importance in social
innovation, is the ability to stand apart from oneself, so to speak,
and perceive oneself as a thinking and emotion-feeling organism.
Persons who have the ability to do this, rather than to assume that
their view of the world is the one true and objective view, also have
the ability to understand the attitudes and reactions of other
persons, and thereby to adapt social institutions to new situations
and achieve social advance.

The history of the later Middle Ages and the early modern era
demonstrates fairly convincingly, it seems to me, that, in comparison with the Continental societies, far more individuals in
Britain, in all social classes except the serfs and not fully free
cultivators, possessed these abilities. In their struggles with each
other for power, the English nobility and most English kings
showed not only self-trust and resourcefulness but also an empathy
for each other's views. This can be deduced, not from their
statements, but from their actions. Moreover, the growing middle
classes – not merely their leaders – displayed much greater trust
in their own ability to arrive at judgements in public affairs than
did the corresponding classes on the Continent, and worked resourcefully and effectively to alter institutions in order to transfer
progressively increasing power to control their own political
destinies into their own hands. Furthermore, increasingly they
spoke and acted as representatives of the lower classes down to the
free cultivators. And the upper classes felt an unvoiced understanding of the middle-class attitudes, sufficient to make them
yield steadily to them without extreme measures of resistance.

On the Continent, even into the nineteenth century, not only
peasants but also the members of many urban groups seemed not
to regard themselves as of the proper status to have ideas about
national affairs, even those closely affecting themselves. They were
somewhat like the Middle Eastern peasant after the Second World
War, who, when asked, 'What would your do about your country's
problems if you were the king (or president)?', could reply only,
'Me the king? How can you say such a thing? I am only a peasant.'[1]
Repeatedly during this era these classes in one country or another

1. Lerner (1958, p. 24). I have not quoted the peasant's statement
literally, but only its spirit.

felt a deep sense of wrongful treatment. When their resentment burst bonds, they responded with violence, but often their violence was only a meaningless and hopeless expression of fury, and when their revolt did depose or displace an authoritarian ruler, to a far greater degree than in Britain they merely turned to a rival authoritarian individual or group, in whom for the time being at least they placed trust to act in a more considerate manner. They conceived to a much lesser degree than did the British of entering into decisions themselves.

The leaders of various noble or middle classes who were more bold in their world views did not conceive of evolving institutions so that the society as a whole would run smoothly. Rather, they thought only in terms of seizing power. When they did so they tended either to be grossly corrupt and self-serving, with no concept of the national welfare as broader than their own (as in Sweden), or to cling compulsively in the face of changed circumstances to organization and procedures which they had inherited from other times (as in the Netherlands).

Consider, first, the development of governmental power in England during the first several centuries after the Conquest.

Precedent existed for the view that the power of the king is absolute. But precedent also existed for the view that the king is subject to law in some sense and to feudal contract with his retainers. British personalities being what they were, the issue did not become one of absolute conflict between these opposing dogmas. Rather, the problem was attacked as a practical one, to be worked out.

In his coronation charter in 1100, Henry I had promised to end the abuses of William II and to 'restore the good government of Edward the Confessor'. These pledges implicitly recognized the subordination of the king's authority to some rule of law or feudal obligations, but they also posed the question with which England wrestled for the next several centuries: since there is no human authority above the king, how can he be prevented from withdrawing at one time what he has offered at another?

The king's agreement could be made absolutely firm only by the gradual definition of a constitution and the ultimate development of moral sanctions which determined that if the king gave orders for unconstitutional ends the troops would not obey. Meanwhile, the king's adherence to the law, whatever that might be understood to be, might be obtained in the first instance because the king himself might feel that he should accommodate himself to the moral pressures upon him, if he felt the pressures from below to be moral ones.

But, in the second place, the moral pressure upon him might be increased by repeated insistence that the king pledge his intentions, in order that his public oath should weigh upon him. Thus in 1215 the barons forced King John to sign the statement of principles of the Great Charter, and, on the average, once every decade they obtained from each king of the next two hundred years a 'confirmation of charters' or reaffirmation of his submission to law. The first two of these kings, Henry III, 1216–1272, and Edward I, 1272–1307, had themselves 'dispensed' from one such pledge each by the pope, but the pressure of public opinion, or some other force, prevented any of the four kings of the next century from the same cynicism. From Henry V and from Henry VI, who together held the throne from 1413 to 1461, only one confirmation of charter was pressed. This, however, was not because they were stronger or more recalcitrant than the preceding monarchs, but because the battle had been largely won.

Third, the growing threads of precedent might be strengthened by codifying the law and writing it down, so that all concerned might know what was the expected practice. There were seven or eight compilations in the last twenty-five years of the reign of Henry I (1100–1135). In the last quarter of the century, Glanvill's great work appeared, and at the mid-point of the thirteenth century, Bracton's. It would not do to suggest that their main purpose was to confine the actions of the king, but neither would it be judicious to assume that this result was not one of the ends consciously or 'intuitively' in the minds of the codifiers.

A fourth enforcement effort of the resourceful barons was to establish machinery by which to supervise the actions of the king. Chapter 61 of the Great Charter provided for supervision of the king's actions by a committee of the barons selected by the barons. A king who agreed to work with such a council might later withdraw his agreement, if he was powerful enough. More than once, the king did.

But the king's behaviour might further be confined by, fifth, financial sanctions, if the king was obdurate. These also depended on acceptance and precedent. The king had his own lands and his own sources of funds from those lands and from various levies to which he had traditional right without approval by his Great Council. But arbitrary kings also tended to be ambitious or extravagant ones who needed extra money. In a country in which the force of precedent, the king's own sense of what was feasible and right, or the power of the barons, prevented the king from arbitrarily extending his powers, the Great Council might then extract a bargain. And so, in 1258, the Great Council refused to grant Henry III the money he needed to carry on his campaigns in France unless he agreed to let the government be carried on in his name by great officers and committees responsible to the Great Council. Henry needed the money, and was forced to agree. This single action did not establish the principle. But the Great Council persisted. In 1309 Edward II obtained a grant of taxes only after accepting conditions concerning his actions. In 1339–40, 1344, and 1348, acceptance of reforms was obtained from Edward III before he was granted money. And so on thereafter. Gradually it became customary that redress of grievances should be agreed to by the king before taxes were granted.

Kings who found their own traditional sources of funds sufficient, or were able to extend them by the widest interpretation of ambiguous rules, could act independently of the Great Council. The next step was to restrict even this power. The feudal principle of the thirteenth century had been merely that every class must sanction its own tax. Under this principle, wool duties were extracted fairly easily by the king from the wool merchants, who perhaps feared some restrictions on their quasi-monopoly if they did not agree, and who, in any event, could deduct the added cost from the prices they paid the wool-growers. If this and the king's other sources of finances had been enough, perhaps parliament would not have been able to find a way of restricting him. But during the Hundred Years' War these levies were not enough, and parliament seized the opportunity offered. Three times during Edward III's reign, when he asked for additional grants, parliament laid down as a condition that no charge or aid of any sort should be levied by him except with the consent of parliament. To obtain the funds, and presumably also because he had no plans for the unreasonable use of funds and saw no difficulty in obtaining grants for reasonable purposes, Edward agreed, and a further restrictive precedent began to be established.

Under Edward III, parliament went further. Surprised at the amounts of money that Edward requested to prosecute his wars, parliament suspected waste or diversion of funds. In fact there was none. Edward was quite willing to let parliament find this out for itself by electing a treasurer to collect and disburse the money. So arose the precedent that was the forerunner of complete control by parliament of governmental appropriations.

In all of these measures, the king and parliament usually accommodated themselves to each other, though with some tension. But it takes two to reach an accommodation and, in the rare cases in which an English king attempted to place himself above the growing body of precedent by the use of force, the nobles accepted the necessity of war or the threat of war. This was the last and ultimate sanction. It was formal notification by the barons of their intention to revolt in defence of their feudal rights that forced King John to accept the Great Charter. He was ready to put the issue to the test of arms, but before he could mobilize a counter-force he died. Almost half a century later, in 1261, the barons again used the ultimate sanction, and took to arms when Henry III attempted to replace the supervisory committee appointed by the Great Council with officials of his own appointment. In 1264, Simon de Montfort took over control of the government in the name of the barons. But Henry was not deposed. Not only could the barons see a remedy to arbitrary royal rule short of arbitrary overthrow; they were sensible enough to know that they needed a king, and a legitimized one. In 1265, Simon had been so far ahead of his time as formally to include knights and burgesses in the parliament. Partly for this reason, some nobles opposed him and rallied to the side of Henry's son, Edward I, and Edward was victorious in battle over Simon de Montfort's forces. But he in his turn was willing to reach an accommodation. While rejecting parliamentary control of the administrative machinery, he accepted the financial reforms asked for by parliament.

Thereafter until the days of the stiff-necked Stuarts there was no need for measures more radical than control of the purse to obtain the king's acquiescence to the growing body of custom that was coming to be known as the nation's constitution.

By a similar process of accommodation, the nobles in their turn gradually accepted the representatives of the middle classes as partners in the exercise of governmental power. The knights and burgesses were first called to the Great Council in the twelfth and thirteenth centuries to report local facts and sometimes also to hear decisions that affected them. The knights and burgesses merged at these meetings, the parliament that was gradually forming thus coming to have two houses rather than three or four. Adams (1935, p. 195) states that they merged because the burghers and gentry felt at home together. The significance of this statement should not be overlooked. That the landed leaders and the new representatives of commerce and finance should feel at home together implies in both an ability to empathize with an alien group that was strikingly absent on the Continent.

Conciliatory Edward I, when he had defeated the reformist baronial group, nevertheless called the knights and burgesses to meetings of the Great Council to approve taxes touching on themselves, under the old feudal principle which was now working new results. They were not yet formally or as of right members of the parliament. But in the fifteenth century, first the Lancastrians and then the Yorkists turned to the Commons to strengthen their popular support, and addressed the Commons as representing the entire country. Edward IV, 1461–1483, drew the gentry into active positions in the government.

There followed the use of parliament by the Tudors to unify the nation. Henry VII, 1485–1509, depended on the adoption of acts by both houses of parliament to give a sure base to property settlements ending the Wars of the Roses, to measures of improvement in governmental administration, to acts forbidding enclosures, and to various other measures. Henry VIII legitimized his separation from Rome by obtaining the approval of parliament to each successive step. And Elizabeth, the great unifier, even though she was always jealous of encroachment on royal prerogatives, greatly strengthened parliament by depending on it to enact her measures of compromise and accommodation.

When James I and Charles I, stubborn and short-sighted, attempted to restore old prerogatives, parliament used its financial power to preserve its rights both to determine the validity of the election of its members and to criticize the royal administration and the royal conduct of foreign affairs. Then, seeking broader guarantees against retrogression, parliament refused money to Charles I until he signed a Petition of Right by which he agreed to abjure arbitrary taxation, arbitrary imprisonment, and the billeting of troops, and – judiciously chosen words which indicated parliament's understanding of both the vagueness and the profound importance of the accommodation that was gradually being worked out – not to extend his prerogative 'beyond the just symetry which maketh a sweet harmony of the whole'.

Parliament was entirely ready to resort to revolutionary means if others would not serve to preserve the constitutional status. Thus in 1629, early in the reign of Charles I, members of the Commons held the Speaker in his chair, to prevent his adjourning the session, while the Commons passed resolutions defining the limits of the king's rights. And ultimately, in 1642, finding no remedy short of force, parliament quite illegally raised an army without the king's signature, in order to wage civil war against him.

If the nation had been fairly well united against the king, war would not have been necessary. The degree of national consensus which had prevailed on many previous issues broke down on that most emotional of questions, religious dogma. But even in an age of intense religious feeling, establishing a governmental dictatorship to enforce the true way of salvation on disbelievers seemed wrong even to Cromwell. The Protectorate withered away in the face of the nation's attitudes. When the monarchy was restored, in spite of the social reaction that accompanied the restoration, the king was unable to regain the powers which his predecessors had gradually yielded, and representative government, like liberty, continued to broaden down from precedent to precedent. In the eighteenth century the Hanoverians attempted to restore the royal power by the use of instruments thoroughly consonant with the crassness of the age, patronage and bribery, but the development of popular representative government was only temporarily retarded.

There was one important qualification to be noted concerning the trend. The view that all classes possessed the capacity to exercise judgement in national affairs and that the attitudes and views of all should be accommodated did not extend to the serfs and the not fully free cultivators, nor, after the end of serfdom, to their successors the copyholders. They were regarded as classes to be ruled, not accepted into participation in government. Until modern times, they probably regarded themselves in the same way. When the serfs felt too great a sense of oppression, in 1381 and again in 1450, they rebelled in desperation. In the one case their rebellion hardly had any realistic purposes. In the other their demand was for improvements in their economic situation, not for a voice in the government. The class excluded was significant numerically: even in the seventeenth century the copyholders, successors to the not fully free cultivators, held one-third of all agricultural land. Their holdings being small, their proportion of the agricultural population must have been larger, so that even at this late date they probably constituted at least a third of the total population. But with this qualification concerning this lowest class, participation in the government was broadened during the centuries from 1200 to 1800 through a notable series of steps of political innovation. That all higher classes thought themselves capable of participation in government, and progressively gained that participation, is a remarkable phenomenon.

Perhaps the most striking aspect is the relative absence among any social group of the view that 'we' are right and 'they' are evil, that the political problem can be solved only if 'we' put 'them' down by force. To put the matter in other words, the remarkable phenomenon is the presence of sufficient creativity in the minds of members of every class to enable them to conceive of the conflicting values and attitudes of other classes as rational and reasonable ones which should be accommodated. A Briton is likely to take so much for granted the social and political change during these centuries that he does not realize how vitally it depended on a degree of creativity that was not common to the other societies of Western Europe. We can appreciate how far from inevitable the British political innovations were by sketching selected highlights of the developments in government in France, the Netherlands, and Sweden during the same era.

At some point between the eleventh and the fourteenth centuries, in each nation of Western Europe, there seems to have been as great a participation in governmental decisions by the nobles, or the nobles, gentry, and merchants, as existed in Britain. But then, as national power was consolidated, the participation failed to increase, or even was reduced.

In France, in the thirteenth century, assemblies of the king's vassals held now and then gave some sort of sanction to the king's policies. The first well-authenticated Estates-General met in 1302. It was called primarily to ensure or demonstrate national support for Philip IV in his conflict with the pope. It included representatives of the towns in their feudal capacity, as did many assemblies called during the two succeeding decades by Philip and his two immediate successors.

Later, the expenses of the Hundred Years' War provided a lever by which the nobles might extract concessions from the king, just as they did in England. In 1346, the year of the battle of Crécy, the cost of the war led the Estates-General of Langue d'Oïl to make reforms the condition of a financial grant to Philip VI. He acquiesced sufficiently to obtain the money. In 1355, the Estates-General of Languedoc and Langue d'Oïl forced John II to agree to continue the existing practice of consulting with them before making new levies, and to accept supervision of the collection and expenditure of the funds by a commission from the Estates. In 1357, when John had been taken prisoner and Charles (later Charles V) had become regent at the age of eighteen, the Estates obtained his signature to a Great Ordinance by which he agreed to supervision of the levy of taxes and the expenditure of funds by a committee of the Estates-General, to frequent and regular meetings of the Estates-General, and to other reforms, though no other that reduced the traditional royal powers.

The parallel to early constitutional developments in England is striking. But war can be used by a vigorous king as an occasion for an increase in his power, as well as by a council or legislature to curb him. During his reign as king (1364–1380) Charles V dominated the supervisory committee chosen by the Estates-General. Then he came to dominate the Estates-General also. In 1360, to ransom John, the Estates-General of Langue d'Oïl authorized a levy to continue for a term of six years, and in 1363 authorized a hearth-tax without time-limit. On the basis of these precedents, Charles induced the Estates to agree that any levy once authorized could be continued indefinitely unless altered. Then the Estates agreed to the transfer of financial control from the Estates-General's committee to a royal financial agency of a century's standing, the *chambre de compte*. The Estates thus gave away without protest or resistance their only important functions, and their only checks upon the powers of the king.

In the fourteenth century, a salt tax had been introduced. By the first half of the fifteenth century, the firmly established right of the king to levy this tax, feudal aides, and the land tax known as the *taille* from which nobles and clergy were exempt, gave him the power to finance almost any measures he chose to undertake. At the one meeting of the Estates-General during the reign of Louis XI (1461–1483), that body asked the king to rule without them in the future. In 1614, under Louis XIII, occurred the last meeting of the Estates-General for 174 years, until national crisis forced Louis XVI to call one in the fateful year 1788. The nobles of the court became 'kept' men.

After the end of the sixteenth century, the only remaining resistance to the king's power was by the non-court nobles and – less forceful – by some of the towns. Perhaps almost half of the nobles were Huguenots towards the end of the sixteenth century, and the Huguenot nobles resisted royal domination. Richelieu crushed them between 1625 and 1630, and in 1648–53 Mazarin destroyed the last nobility opposing the king by arms. In these actions Richelieu and Mazarin also weakened a source of strength to the country, but that by some accommodation they might preserve the contribution of the nobles did not occur to them, or at least not to their sovereign.

In the cities, and especially in Paris, local 'courts' or *parlements* had long attempted to assert partial legislative powers – something like a judicial review of the king's decrees. These *parlements* consisted of nobles as well as capitalists, and, indeed, the 1648–53 action of Mazarin was against a noble-capitalist *Fronde* centring in Paris. These local attempts at some independence persisted for a further period, but failed.

There is ample evidence of independence of spirit among the artisans, merchant-capitalists, and some non-court nobles in France over the period from the sixteenth to the eighteenth century. The Huguenot movement, among both the noble and the non-noble classes, is in itself evidence enough. The fairly vigorous economic growth of these centuries provides corroborative testimony. It is, of course, identified with the Huguenots, but there was also participation in it by many individuals from non-Huguenot groups. These groups were sufficiently innovational and sufficiently orientated towards manual-technical and economic achievement for it to be said that, if the national environment had been hospitable rather than hostile, an industrial revolution might have occurred in France as early as in England. Why, then, did they not succeed in bringing about the liberalization of government that occurred in Britain?

The main answer, it seems to me, lies in the absence of that capacity of one group to empathize with another which was so conspicuous a characteristic of English social life.

In the first place, the kings felt little responsibility for the welfare of the country. From the fourteenth century on, national unity grew, but the kings, from then until the Revolution four hundred years later, consistently regarded the country as a feudal noble might regard his fief: as a piece of property, a possession, rather than an organism for which they had some responsibility or to which they had an obligation. If one pictures Elizabeth I as queen of France, one can imagine the differences in policy that might have ensued.

And the attitude of the kings was mirrored, in less extreme form, in that of many other groups. The reason the opportunity for the development of representative government presented by the kings' needs during the Hundred Years' War was missed, says one standard historian of the period, is that 'as the bourgeoisie and nobility distrusted each other, no effective measures were taken and no permanent constitutional development took place'.[1] The gentry held the bourgeoisie in disdain, and the bourgeoisie returned the contempt. That the two should merge in one legislative body, or intermarry, as they did in England, was inconceivable. The bourgeoisie, in their turn, could not organize a broad base of power among the common people, because they looked with disdain upon the common people, and in various communities they formed themselves into oligarchies. In the mid-fourteenth century, it is true, that extraordinary merchant, Étienne Marcel, richest man in Paris and leader of the Estates-General of Langue d'Oïl, intrigued not only with the revolting peasants but also with the English. Perhaps this was a counsel of desperation, justified by the absence of other bases of power. In any event, he succeeded only in discrediting the merchants.

The contrast between the English and French civil wars in the fifteenth century will illustrate the difference in the flavours of the two cultures. In the Wars of the Roses, though there was probably somewhat greater popular sympathy for the Yorkists than for the Lancastrians, in the main the two sides fought battles rather

---

1. Paul Cram, in Langer (ed.), *An encyclopaedia of world history*, p. 232. Cram's remark refers specifically to the reign of Philip IV, 1285–1314, but it is clear from the context that it is equally applicable to the rest of that century and the next.

removed from the lives of the common people. The wars were brought to an end by a union of sorts between the two families, and the reigns of reconciliation of the first Tudors. In the wars between the reactionary Armagnacs and the pro-English Burgundians, the victory of the Armagnacs in 1413 led to feudal reaction and the suppression of all reform, and the recapture of power by the Burgundians five years later was followed by a massacre of Armagnacs. The final end of the rivalry was the destruction of the Burgundians by arms by Louis XI, one step in the establishment of absolute monarchy. Neither reconciliation between the two groups nor any responsibility to popular desires or emotions was thought relevant.

It is inconceivable that successive Great Councils or parliaments in England would have agreed passively to the progressive destruction of the right of the classes they represented to participate in political decisions. English nobles were able to unite, the gentry and the merchants were able to make common cause with each other, and all three groups were able to co-operate when it served to advance their participation in governmental affairs. Only dogmatic differences caused a civil war, and after this one spasm of violence all concerned saw that this would not do. In France, none of the comparable groups except the Huguenot nobles and the merchants could enter into the necessary mutual accommodation. The other groups and the kings had no conception that life permitted such a phenomenon. The kings and the nobles had no conception that their view of the world was something different from the objective nature of the world itself, that their values had a subjective rather than an absolute origin. Speaking broadly, and ignoring exceptional individuals who were too few and too deviant to be influential, throughout these several centuries each of the relatively elite groups thought of other groups simply as objects, to be used; and of groups with values conflicting with theirs as either evil or viciously misguided, and to be humbled. The creativity that might have conceived of the values of other groups as having meaning, and of the conflicts of view as a problem to be solved by mutual accommodation, was lacking. This persisting difference in personality, rather than merely the external circumstances, seems to me the main key to the difference in the historical trend in the two societies from the later Middle Ages to the eighteenth century.

In the Netherlands a high degree of technical creativity manifested itself up to the sixteenth century, if not later, and the country showed great vigour in other fields during the seventeenth century. The economic record has been summarized above (p. 38). In the revolt of the separate Netherlands provinces against Spain, from 1566 on, the Dutch could not match the Spanish land forces, but the irregular sea forces known as the Sea Beggars controlled the waters, captured the important towns in the states of Holland and Zeeland, and led those states into revolt. The town councils alleged that King Philip's general, Alva, had abused the king's confidence, and declared William of Orange to be Philip's lieutenant in his absence. Thus they both legalized the revolt and quieted fears that it was a Calvinist theocratic movement. This brilliant tactic permitted the Catholic leaders of the southern provinces to join with those of the north in the 'Pacification of Ghent'. All agreed that they would first eject the Spanish troops and then settle their religious differences at a States-General. The Catholic-led southern provinces, however, soon ceased their revolt, after receiving concessions from Spain; but in the north, under a military genius, the Dutch won victories even on land and, with the aid of England, gained *de facto* independence in 1609, which received formal sanction in the treaty of Westphalia of 1648.

In the text above, the term Netherlands has denoted both the northern and the southern provinces. In discussing events after independence, I shall use it to signify the independent northern provinces only, and shall refer to the people of these provinces as the Dutch. Holland was the largest and the single most important state.

In the seventeenth century the seafarers turned to colonization. Batavia was founded in 1619. The Portuguese were driven from Malacca and from Ceylon. The Dutch established themselves at the Cape of Good Hope in 1652, in Sumatra in 1657, and in Angola during the same period. Between 1623 and 1661 they established a Dutch colony in northern Brazil.

This economic and political flowering was matched by an efflorescence in art and literature.

Why were the groups that demonstrated creativity in these various ways unwilling to develop institutions of representative government in the seventeenth and eighteenth centuries, and unable to carry forward their technical progress? A central part of the answer is that certain rigid elements in their view of the world made it impossible for them either to reach the internal accommodations that would have brought national unity or to modify the institutions and activities that had been rewarding in the different circumstances of previous generations.

During the first half of the sixteenth century, when Henry VIII was creating a spirit of national pride in England, the history of the Netherlands is one of a series of stiff-necked bitter conflicts between Catholics and Calvinists; the clergy and the laity; the towns and the country gentry; one town and another; the provinces and the central bureaucracy. When one thinks of the unifying leadership of Henry VIII and then later of Elizabeth, one realizes what might have happened in the Netherlands if a different spirit had existed among the people.

After independence, the tiny states and the towns continued to be compulsively localist. Though the problems of military and naval defence and economic organization cried out to be solved by national union, Holland and Zeeland had contempt for the land provinces and would not surrender an iota of their particularistic authority. Neither would Holland surrender any bit of the hegemony which by her economic strength she exerted over the other provinces.

And each state was oligarchical, not democratic. The country as a whole was ruled, it has been estimated, by some ten thousand oligarchs: city aristocrats of trade and a few country nobles. The town councils, the state assemblies, and the government offices became virtually closed corporations. After 1650, explicit contracts were made among leading families to divide and rotate the lucrative offices. Some members of the ruling class bought country estates, to obtain the titles associated with them. The oligarchies, it is true, were in the main benevolent, but nevertheless authoritarian, and too concerned with their economic and symbolic prerogatives to make even the adaptations that might have permitted those prerogatives to continue.

In the eighteenth century, the groups in power in the sea provinces continued to dream of the sea power which had brought their ancestors glory as their key to the perpetuation of world position. Yet they clung rigidly to other prerogatives which prevented the practical measures necessary for the preservation of sea power. The oligarchs of the sea provinces pursued wholesale disarmament and economy, and Vlekke suggests that this was because the maintenance of naval strength would have required them to impose some taxes on themselves. After 1750, opposing factions in the States-General preferred the army and the navy respectively, and, being unable to reach a compromise, let both decline. The long decline in Dutch shipping and colonial power continued.

During the seventeenth and eighteenth centuries, the common citizens of the towns, as well as the cultivators, passively accepted oligarchical rule. The city guards (police) of the towns and the armed men of the House of Orange were drawn from the oligarchs. The commoners could have overthrown the oligarchs at any time without bloodshed. There is no plausible explanation of their failure to demand participation in the town governments except that they were unable to visualize themselves as sharing in decisions. To put the matter simply, the idea rarely occurred to them, and when it did it seemed a bold and pleasant fantasy, which they might mention, but not insist on. At times of great frustration they revolted, but, when they did, in the classic manner they merely transferred their allegiance from one set of authoritarian rulers to another.

One national official, with little more than formal duties in peacetime, existed. This was the *stadhouder*, that is, 'place-holder' or lieutenant. The office was a survival of the time when the states had owed allegiance to a foreign ruler, who had appointed a resident representative in each. After independence, the office was somewhat anomalous, but it was continued, perhaps largely because of inertia and because its abolition would have been a slight on the nobles who were the *stadhouders* at the time. Then, it did become a vehicle for paying respect to the house which had been the early leader of the independence movement, the House of Orange. After independence, most states, but excluding Holland and some others, followed the practice of choosing the same person, the Prince of Orange or of Nassau-Orange, as *stadhouder*. The office preserved a thread of at least symbolic unity among some of the states, and, in time of war, some degree of unity in the command of the armed forces might be achieved by turning that command over to a common *stadhouder*.

In a crisis in 1672, when the Netherlands were at war with France and England, the urban masses of Holland revolted, and forced the oligarchs to make William of Orange, already *stad-*

houder of most other states, *stadhouder* of Holland as well. The city guards and guilds then asked for representation in the States-General. William decided against this and, when he had announced his decision, the matter rested.

Again in 1747, when France invaded the Netherlands, a revolt of the middle and lower classes forced the oligarchs to make William of Nassau-Orange *stadhouder* of every state, commander-in-chief of the army and navy, and director-in-chief of the failing East and West India companies. This was the first time that every state had elected the same man as *stadhouder*, much less given him the other executive powers indicated. The city guards then drew up a programme of reforms. William responded by replacing some officials and altering the customs duties, but he let die proposals for a central executive body and additional representatives in the States-General. And the revolting classes took no further action.

In the 1790s, the French Revolutionaries put *émigré* Dutch 'patriots' in power in the Netherlands. The 'patriots' barred the nobility from membership in state assemblies, abolished the office of *stadhouder*, ended provincial sovereignty – and then demonstrated the purely verbal quality of their innovational abilities by debating the proper degree of centralization for several years until the French army, its patience exhausted, imposed the French constitution of 1795. After 1800, Netherlands nationalist feeling turned to the House of Orange for leadership. An Orangist of the oligarchy took command. His proclamation indicates both the oligarchy's view of the common people and the (quite correct) oligarchical evaluation of the strength of the popular demand for self-government. 'All leading people', he proclaimed, 'will have a part in the new government; the common people will have a holiday with entertainment at public expense' (Vlekke, 1945, p. 286). William VI, who became king, decided the form of the new constitution. He vested most power over taxation in himself, and laid down requirements for the franchise which limited it to a tiny proportion of the population. How small that fraction was is indicated by the fact that a further reform in 1848, which greatly extended the franchise, gave it to between 6 and 7 per cent of adults. Popular representative government developed in a series of steps between that date and 1917.

The historian Vlekke (1945, p. 272) writes of the eighteenth

century as a whole: 'Action always lagged far behind the roar of
oratorical protest. The absurd contrast between the energy spent
in words and that spent in deeds was so great that often, as in
1747 and 1787, the effect is tragi-comical.'

One is justified in concluding that the proximate cause of the
fatal Dutch localism during the seventeenth and eighteenth centuries was the compulsive adherence to obsolete and 'dysfunctional'
values by elite local groups, and that the immediate explanation
of this adherence is simply that the localist view was so built into
personality that rational considerations were disregarded. One may
conclude also that the failure to adopt an institutional framework
which would have permitted the middle classes to continue their
contributions to national progress, technical and other, was the
rigid short-sightedness of the elite groups combined with the utter
lack of self-trust in political matters of the bourgeoisie. In Dutch
history, as in French, personality deserves an explicit place as a
causal variable.

Lastly, consider Sweden, the other country where the early
stream of technical innovation might have led to an industrial
Revolution by the eighteenth century. As in France and the
Netherlands, conspicuous features of the nation's history are class
hostility and the lack of self-trust of the middle classes.

In the eleventh century, the hitherto entirely separate provinces
of Sweden recognized a common king, though one with little
central power. Social distinctions sharpened. By the thirteenth
century, four estates were recognized: nobles, bishops, burghers,
and peasant landowners. The gentry, that is, the younger sons of
the noble families, allied themselves with their families. This, it
will be remembered, was the century in which, when the English
king called the gentry and burghers to meet with him, they formed
a common body, because 'they felt at home together'. And the
English bishops and nobles had long been fused politically, in the
Great Council. In Sweden, the four classes held themselves rigidly
separate from each other.

The period from the late fourteenth to the early sixteenth
century was a period of continuing tension concerning the country's
relationship to Denmark. The great nobles allied themselves with
the king of Denmark in fighting for union, largely because when
there was no Swedish king, they, the great nobles, ruled Sweden.
A group of nationalist nobles, supported by many peasants,

burghers, and a middle class of tax-exempt miners, fought for independence. Periods of union and of independence alternated. However, during the periods of non-union, the peasants, burghers, and miners did not participate in the government. The king or the nationalist nobles ruled.

When Gustavus Adolphus became king in 1611, he agreed not to legislate or tax except with the consent of the Council of nobles and bishops or of the national legislature, the *Riksdag* – but agreed not to call many *Riksdags*. The *Riksdag* consisted of the four estates meeting separately. Any one estate could veto any measure, but, in practice, this provision meant merely that the higher classes could block any move towards reduction of their power. Gustavus Adolphus agreed also that the important and privileged offices of governmental administration should be held only by nobles.

The Council dominated the government after Gustavus Adolphus's death in 1632. After half a century of arbitrary noble rule and long wars, rebellion swept the country in 1682. However, the revolting groups made no demand for a voice in the government. Rather, they gave hearty approval when a strong king assumed absolute power.

A generation later, reaction against arbitrary kingly rule returned power to the *Riksdag* and Council. But in the *Riksdag* the nobles set up a 'secret committee' to handle delicate matters – which meant any matter that they referred to it – and denied the peasants membership on the committee. The reaction of the peasants was to demand the return of powers to the king. The response of the other estates was to legislate penalties on the peasants for their insubordination.

In 1772, following fifty years of flagrantly corrupt government by two conflicting parties of nobles which alternately gained power, King Gustav seized power by a military coup. While the army watched, the *Riksdag* adopted a constitution giving him the initiative in legislation, war, and the administration of justice, and a large measure of independent financing. He agreed to consult with the Council about his measures. The public rejoiced at this curtailment of the *Riksdag*'s power. Even the need to consult irked Gustav, and he obtained further legislative change which gave him complete legislative power and control of the membership of the Council. Ironically, the year in which this regression occurred was 1789. France was far away.

In 1809, by a military-civil coup, Gustav was deposed and the power of the king reduced. But not until 1865 was there an extension of representation in the *Riksdag* (which became bi-cameral), and even then the property qualification for voting was such that far less than one-fourth of adult males had the vote.[1] Only in 1909, after agitation by industrial workers, was universal suffrage adopted.

In Sweden, as in France and the Netherlands, it seems fair to state that two qualities characterized behaviour during the later Middle Ages and even down to 1800. First, each group in power viewed its own attitudes and interests as right, and the desires of other groups merely as interferences. None could conceive of the existence of attitudes and interests conflicting with its own as reasonable, and regard it as reasonable to seek mutual accommodation with them. Second, the social groups without political power did not act to gain it. To state that they were not powerful enough to gain participation in the government is simply wrong; on a number of occasions, their rebellion was the key factor in the overthrow of the government in power. And to state that they were not resourceful enough to rearrange institutions so as to gain power is true, but misleading. No doubt they were not sufficiently resourceful, but this is not the main reason they achieved no participation in government. The record surely suggests that the reason is that they did not think of themselves as fit to participate. (Indeed, because their sense of their proper status prevented their minds from functioning in the field of government, they were not fit.) Even in 1800, peasants, artisans, merchants, and all, they were still saying, 'I, a mere peasant? How can I know . . .?'

In summary, even these cavalierly brief references to the history of England, France, the Netherlands, and Sweden during the later Middle Ages and the early modern era indicate fairly clearly two contrasts in personality (which have been mentioned several times above). A shorthand way of describing these contrasts is as follows: First, whereas the English–Welsh people creatively resolved their social conflicts, each of the three Continental peoples merely fought about them. Second, the middle classes of England and Wales trusted their own judgement in political affairs,

1. In 1890, after continuing inflation had greatly reduced the real value of the property requirement, an estimated one-fourth of adult males could vote.

and pressed resourcefully and persistently (and successfully) for increasing participation in government.[1] This self-trust was largely lacking on the Continent.[2]

These difficulties in personality, I suspect, greatly influenced the history of these countries. Governmental structure in the three Continental countries developed differently from that in England, not merely because the peoples concerned faced different circumstances, but because they were characterized by differing personalities.

Parallel conclusions could, I think, be drawn from an analysis of the developments in religious organization and belief in the four countries, but the analysis is too complex to be referred to here, even in summary form.[3]

In laying stress in this paper on personality differences, I do not intend to imply that they have been left unmentioned by historians: 'national character' or 'the spirit of the age', which is to say, personality, is mentioned in many historical accounts. Rarely, however, has it been given much analysis as a force independent of the circumstances impinging on individuals from the outside.

In one view, it has been regarded as an 'intervening variable', brought about in a way that an intelligent layman can readily perceive by the historical or physical circumstances of the society. Such explanation is often plausible. The spectacular success of the naval activity of the sea provinces of the Netherlands, acting quite separately from the other provinces, during the fight for independence, may be a cause of the overriding value placed on local autonomy by later generations in those provinces. Germany's lack of clearly defined and readily defended national boundaries during

1. I refer at times to England and Wales, or to the English and Welsh, rather than to Britain or the British, because both the Industrial Revolution and, in the main, the political development sketched here occurred in England and Wales, not in Scotland.

2. When it is lacking, representative government is not the best system of government. The analysis suggests that representative government is the best form, not universally, but where and when, scattered among the masses of the people, there are a sufficient number of individuals who trust their own judgement.

3. It does not consist merely of an application of Weber's 'Protestant ethic' thesis. While there are many suggestive insights in Weber's great work, his conception of a line of causation running in a rather simple and direct fashion from religious belief to economic behaviour is not persuasive.

the historical period in which nation-states arose may have created a fear of her neighbours which, in turn, bred a high degree of aggressiveness into German personality. But this is the sort of layman's reasoning that suggested, before the days of modern medical knowledge, that exposure to night air causes epidemics since, as everyone knows, night air is colder and damper than day-time air, and cold and damp breed disease. On reflection, it often becomes clear after reading historical explanations of personality that opposite qualities of personality, if they had existed, could have been explained with equal plausibility.

Another view, then, is that, since personality differences among societies are inexplicable, discussion of them contributes little to historical explanation.

That personality differences are still largely inexplicable is undoubtedly true. If conditions in the society at large do affect the values and motives of the individual, what are the precise mechanisms by which they do so? Why is it that precepts urged by the elders and stressed in formal education more often than not are highly valued by the next generation, but sometimes are rejected?

Only the psycho-analytical analysis of personality seems likely to give much aid in answering such questions. And one of the early contributions of this analysis, unfortunately, is to destroy the simplicity of one common-sense assumption, namely, that educa-tion largely determines values. For psycho-analysis indicates that the emotions and actions of an individual's parents, or, more generally, of all the persons important to him in his early years, play a greater part in determining his attitudes and values than do the verbal precepts they urge upon him. More precisely, the emotional atmosphere of infancy and childhood is of the utmost importance in determining the child's reaction to the precepts presented to him. The following generalizations, though uncertain and needing a great deal of qualification, undoubtedly contain a large element of truth. If the parents' and other elders' role in life is satisfying to *them*, and their relationship to the infant and child is satisfying to *him*, he will tend to accept their model, and the wisdom they preach, and when he is older not depart from either. But if the unease of the parents makes it obvious to the infant and child that their role in life is not satisfying to them, or if the emotional tensions they are experiencing cause them to create an environment which is unsatisfying in certain ways to the infant and child, then he may reject the relevant aspects of their model, and of their wisdom, no matter how sincerely and earnestly they preach it.

More generally, psycho-analytical theory causes us to believe that all aspects of personality, including the degree of creativity and the attitudes that influence the field in which it will be exercised, are rooted early in life, even though also influenced by all later experiences; and that, among the early influences, the parents' and others' unconscious or automatic reactions to the child, and the model their lives and emotions present, often speak to him so loudly that he cannot hear the words they preach to him.

All of this should make us extremely wary of lay analysis of the impact of history on personality. Yet except for some bold speculations which have a technical basis but go so far beyond it that at best they are highly uncertain,[1] there is no professional analysis of the impact of history on personality. However, what little is known should impress historians with the fact that personality in a society during any era may be an important causal factor independent of the external circumstances of that era; a factor whose origins are not yet understood, but one which ought to be taken into account as co-ordinate in influence with the country's wars, the progress of knowledge, etc.

If one accepts this principle, one may draw the following three conclusions about the probable relationship of personality differences to the technical progress of England and the Continental countries during the early modern era.

First, if the differential development of governmental institutions in the four countries leads one to admit the possibility of personality differences, the presence of personality differences must also be accepted as a *possible* explanatory hypothesis in analysing the differential rate of technical progress. Once it is accepted as a possible explanatory hypothesis, it seems to me to account quite neatly for some phenomena which are otherwise explained only with considerable strain. To assume personality differences may, of course, be a cheap way out of every historical problem: 'Why did country A do better than country B?' 'Well, perhaps the people of A were more creative.' But that a thesis can be thus abused does not constitute a valid reason for not considering it carefully.

1. I would classify my own theorizing in my book *On the theory of social change* in this category.

Second, if, in their governmental advance, the English and Welsh manifested a more widespread presence of self-trust than did the Continental peoples considered here, some presumption is created that they also possessed more self-trust, hence more creativity, in the technical field. The two are not necessarily associated, but a presumption does exist. Satisfaction in the exercise of one's autonomous judgement about affairs of importance to one (a definition of self-trust) is an essential ingredient in both. One would therefore expect economic growth and movement from authoritarian towards representative government typically to be associated. A survey of the developing societies of the world provides evidence that, in fact, typically they are.[1]

However, there are important and conspicuous exceptions, for example, the Soviet Union and Japan. In both, authoritarianism persisted in the governmental sphere while rapid progress occurred in the technical sphere. The authoritarian government in these countries was a creative solution of a political problem in this sense: in each case, the authoritarian government (*a*) removed institutional obstacles to economic progress and (*b*) acted on behalf of the entire society, rather than merely on behalf of a limited social group. The preservation of forms of government characterized by many traditional features seems to be a device by which the self-reliant individuals of some societies have freed their energies for innovation in other fields, including the technical. More generally, an individual may give himself the emotional security necessary for bold innovation in one area of activity by being highly traditional in other areas. Thus he protects his psychological flanks, so to speak. Moreover, one area may be of interest to him and other areas not. If so, he may be an innovator in the one area, and not wish to waste energy thinking about other areas.

Yet persisting class rigidities – weakness of concern by influential groups for anything but their own current status – do seem to reflect such a constricted personality quality that there is some presumption that they indicate limited creativity in other fields as well.

Of course, the oligarchs might be rigidly self-centred and compulsively attached to old forms while other groups were innovational. Indeed, this must have been the case in each of the three

1. For the evidence, see the essay by Coleman which constitutes the last chapter of Almond and Coleman (1960).

Continental countries, for otherwise the relatively vigorous technical progress in France and Sweden during the several centuries preceding 1700, and in the Netherlands up to at least 1600, cannot be explained. But, deprived of the energy of the leading socio-economic groups, technical innovation weakened, and failed to keep pace with that in England and Wales.[1]

Third, oligarchic or royal resistance to change, plus pre-occupation with the preservation of old prerogatives, hampered the development in the three Continental countries of economic institutions fostering technical progress, and, of course, in France, also led to the persecution of the Huguenot innovators. The adverse effect of these phenomena is a commonplace of historical analysis, and need not be mentioned further here. The intention of this paper has been rather to emphasize the likelihood that innovational energy was greater in technical matters in England and Wales, not because differential circumstances drew it out, but because at the time the British were a more innovational people.

REFERENCES

ADAMS, GEORGE BURTON (1935) *Constitutional history of England.* (Rev. edn.) London: Jonathan Cape.

ALMOND, G. A. & COLEMAN, J. S. (eds.) (1960) *The politics of the developing areas.* Princeton, N.J.: Princeton University Press.

ANDERSON, HAROLD H. (ed.) (1959) *Creativity and its cultivation.* New York: Harper.

ASHTON, T. S. (1951) *Iron and steel in the industrial revolution.* (2nd edn.) Manchester: Manchester University Press.

1. There does not seem to be any case in which the protection by oligarchies of pre-industrial class rigidities is associated with continuing rapid technical progress. One would need to examine certain cases carefully before making this assertion quite firmly. Argentina is a case in point. In the 1920s, Argentina was among the world's leaders in economic prowess; she is mentioned in some of the literature of that decade alongside the United States, Canada, and Australia. Subsequently, bitter class hostilities and the narrowest of group selfishness have appeared. However, it is probably fair to state that the social myopia that is present today did not develop until well into the twentieth century, and is correlated with the failure of vigorous economic growth in Argentina to continue. If so, then the experience of Argentina is a confirmation of the principle enunciated here rather than an exception to it.

CLAPHAM, SIR JOHN (1949) *A concise economic history of Britain to 1750.* London: Cambridge University Press.

HAGEN, EVERETT E. (1962) *On the theory of social change.* Homewood, Ill.: Dorsey Press; London: Tavistock Publications, 1964.

LANGER, WILLIAM L. (ed.) (n.d.) *An encyclopaedia of world history.* (rev. 3rd edn.) London: Harrap.

LERNER, DANIEL (1958) *The passing of traditional society.* Glencoe, Ill.: Free Press.

SINGER, CHARLES, HOLMYARD, E. J., HALL, A. R. & WILLIAMS, TREVOR R. (eds.) (1957) *A history of technology*, Vol. III: *From the Renaissance to the industrial revolution, c. 1550 to 1750.* Oxford: Clarendon Press.

VLEKKE, B. H. M. (1945) *Evolution of the Dutch nation.* New York: Roy.

The Comparative Analysis of Historical Change[1]

REINHARD BENDIX

The renewed interest in comparative studies of social change dates from World War II. This intellectual repercussion of the war and its aftermath is most apparent in the discontinuities of interest which have marked the work of American social scientists in recent decades. Before World War II American scholars devoted their primary attention to the study of American society. Even if one considers the tremendous popularity of theories of social evolution in the United States before the 1920s, one is struck by the fact that these theories were largely applied in Social Darwinist fashion to an interpretation of the competitive economic struggle. The predominant American concern was domestic, in contrast with the trend in Europe, where these theories originated and where they were used to interpret the encounter between the advanced industrial societies of Europe and the peoples and cultures of colonial and dependent areas. With the notable exception of anthropologists, this intellectual 'insularity' of American social scientists may be related to America's anti-colonial heritage, just as the renewed interest in comparative studies may be related to America's world wide political involvements since World War II.

As a result, the earlier parochial orientation has declined, as economists, political scientists, and sociologists attempt to assess the relativity as well as the characteristics of the American experience. A steadily increasing number of social scientists are concerned with non-Western areas, especially with regard to problems of 'modernization'. This concern has benefited markedly from the

1. Revised version of a paper originally presented to the Round Table on Comparative Research, International Social Science Council, Paris, 22–24 April 1965. The paper develops themes presented in more empirical detail in my book *Nation-building and Citizenship* (1964).

wartime experience of many scholars, including extensive training in foreign languages. It has also been affected by the revolution in research methods that modern computers make possible with regard to the storage and evaluation of data. We seem to find ourselves in a period of intellectual transition, and the participants in this reorientation naturally tend to emphasize its novelty.

The shift of emphasis is evident if one compares the preoccupation of scholars with the conventional teaching of history. Typically, the student learns the history of his own country in considerable detail, whereas the histories of other countries are presented to him much more selectively, or not at all. At one time, professional historians defended this conventional method on the ground that the development of each country is unique, so that the obvious concern with education for citizenship coincided with a plausible, intellectual conviction. Yet today historians no longer adhere to this position as firmly as they did some two generations ago. In notable instances they have presented comparative studies of their own. A series of publications has focused on problems of generalization in historical studies. And while preoccupation with national history remains predominant, many scholars so preoccupied are nevertheless concerned with the questions of conceptualization of central interest to social scientists.[1]

Yet the change in intellectual orientation may be more apparent than real. The greater receptivity towards a conceptual and comparative approach to the study of history is not matched by much agreement on what such a programme of study implies positively. There is little agreement on what is to be understood by such recurrent terms as analysis, change, social structure, and comparison. Taking each in turn, I shall try to indicate the issues involved in our use of these terms. My purpose is to propose an approach to the comparative analysis of historical change at an intermediate level of abstraction.[2]

1. Note the two Bulletins of the Social Science Research Council (1946, 1954), dealing with the relations between history and the social sciences; see also Gottschalk (1963). The statement in the text is especially well illustrated, however, by the many contributions of historians published in the pages of *Comparative Studies in Society and History* (edited by Silvia Thrupp).

2. Though more directly concerned with the study of historical change, the intention here is similar to that of Merton in his discussion of theories of the middle range (see his *Social theory and social structure*, 2nd edn.,

Analysis

At least three divergent approaches to the study of historical change may be distinguished for purposes of orientation. The older, evolutionist approach tended to be classificatory. It assumes that the less developed countries will follow the 'steps and sequences of change' through which the more developed have passed already. Analysis becomes a matter of assigning culture traits or even a whole country at a given time to a specific stage of development. Once this is done, it is possible to assess the progressive or regressive significance of ideas and actions, either because the future or next stage is 'known' in advance, or because it seems plausible to examine the past of the 'developed' countries for purposes of such retrospective evaluation. To be sure, evolutionist theory is no longer expounded in such simplistic terms. Scholars have become more cautious than their predecessors: concepts of differentiation or increasing complexity are substituted for the idea of progress, and allowance is made for multilinear developments and the reversal or omission of 'stages'.[1] But while these modifications go far, it is not clear that the original theory has been abandoned. The proliferation of synonyms of change, such as development or modernization, with their several adjectives, warns us that this is an area of uncertainty and confusion; the new vocabulary often employs older theories of evolution uncritically.

Related to this older approach, but more modern in its nomenclature, is the view that societies should be analysed as 'natural systems'. In this perspective a social structure appears as an interrelated, functioning whole with systemic prerequisites, properties, and consequences, which may be identified as a 'stage of

1. Cf. the recent contributions of Parsons (1964), Bellah (1964), and Eisenstadt (1964). Regrettably, these writers take no note of the important contribution by Watt and Goody, 'The consequences of literacy' (1963). Note also the closely related analysis by Snell, *Scenes from Greek drama* (1964, *passim*). For scholars interested in evolution, these studies have the great advantage of focusing attention on a more or less documented record of transition from a preliterate to a literate society.

1957, pp. 9–10 and *passim*). For certain purposes, higher levels of abstraction may well be useful, and, logically, one cannot speak of intermediate levels of abstraction without acknowledging the existence and possible utility of higher levels as well. However, considerable differences of judgement and emphasis remain with regard to the direct, analytic utility of such higher levels, as the following discussion indicates.

development'. Typically, such analysis runs the danger of reification, which occurs whenever a society is identified as a unit that maintains or changes itself in order to 'survive' as such. I shall comment on this view below, but wish to refer here to one modern tendency which is related to, but not identical with, this wholistic or systemic approach. I refer to the social engineering approach, which is oriented towards planned social change. In this view, analysis should aim at the discovery of critical independent variables, since control of these will entail predictable changes in the dependent variables. Indebted to images derived from controlled experiments or from medical practice, this approach is less classificatory than the older evolutionist theory and less organicist than systems-theory proper. But, like these theories, its simplifying assumptions and tests of truth depend upon a *ceteris paribus* treatment of historical constellations. For example, the record of economic growth in the developed countries is employed as a model, however provisionally, so that historical preconditions reappear as logical prerequisites, without which growth cannot occur. In this way the engineering approach comes close to the 'natural systems' approach in that both operate with the concept of 'indispensable prerequisites', though the engineering approach is perhaps more candid in generalizing from the Western experience.[1]

Comparative analysis of historical change attempts a closer approximation to the historical evidence than is possible on the assumptions of evolutionism, or of systems-theory, or of social engineering. As a result, it promises less in the way of prediction and in the way of guiding social actions towards defined goals. Whether this sacrifice is permanent or temporary remains to be seen. Studies of social change in complex societies may hold in abeyance the tasks of causal analysis and prediction while concentrating on the preliminary task of ordering the phenomena of social change to be analysed further. This task can be characterized

---

1. In a recent contribution, Lerner suggests that, since rising output per head depends especially upon a people's willingness to change, politicians are well advised to promise economic benefits only after people have changed their ways in the requisite direction. He is silent, however, on how politicians can be induced to act in this manner, or on how people are likely to change in the absence of promises, or why in the movements for independence the value of independence has priority over the value of economic growth (cf. Lerner, 1965).

by reference to the meaning of 'change' and of 'social structure'.

Change

At the risk of oversimplification, I shall assume that, at a minimum, considerations of change involve two terminal conditions, so that the word 'change' refers to the differences observed before and after a given interval of time. Since the future is uncertain, studies of historical change deal in the first place with past changes, the better to understand what the contrasts between 'before and after' are and how they have come about. Naturally it is hoped that a better understanding of historical changes will contribute to a fuller exploration of developmental possibilities, perhaps even to constructive action, but the relations between knowledge and action are complex and should not be prejudged.

Studies of change, then, depend upon contrasts between social structures before and after change has occurred. Without knowledge of the respects in which a later social structure differs from an earlier one, we do not know what changes to look for and explain. This is one reason why studies of this kind use familiar concepts such as feudalism, democracy, totalitarianism, etc., despite the many justified criticisms levelled against these terms. Such concepts express something we want to express, namely, that in some overall and important, but rather general, sense, an old social structure has passed away and a new one has taken its place. Dissatisfaction with such conventional terms is understandable, but it is no solution to substitute universal terms for these concepts of limited applicability. In a recent contribution, Almond (Almond & Coleman, 1960, pp. 38–45 and *passim*) has suggested, for example, that 'interest aggregation' is a term that cuts across all the conventional distinctions between political systems and hence can be applied universally. Such a term has the utility of prompting us to look for 'interest aggregation' in unfamiliar social structures to which our conventional terms do not apply, but it does not dispense with the utility of terms such as 'class' or 'estate' which already differentiate – however approximately – the more familiar types of 'interest aggregation'. I suspect that we shall invent new terms to fit the unfamiliar types of 'interest aggregation' once we have analysed them sufficiently, for concepts are the result of inquiry as much as they are its precondition.

What, then, is meant by 'social structures' and how do we study them comparatively?

Social structures

Social structures retain certain of their characteristics while individuals come and go. The specification of such enduring characteristics involves abstractions from observations of behaviour and from historical evidence. On this basis, studies of social change should be able to state that one type of social structure has ceased to prevail and another has taken its place. Yet to make such an assertion involves the hazards demonstrated by the debates concerning Max Weber's ideal type. Definitions of structures such as feudalism, bureaucracy, etc. usually take the form of enumerating several distinguishing characteristics. Such enumerations necessarily 'freeze' the fluidity of social life, as Weber himself emphasized. They say nothing about the strength or generality with which a given characteristic must be present, nor do they say anything about structures in which one or another element of the definition is missing. The result has been uncertainty. Abstractions are needed to define the characteristics of a structure and thus they remove the definition from the evidence. On the other hand, when we approach the evidence 'definition at hand', we often find its analytic utility diminished, because the characteristics to which it refers are in fact neither unequivocal nor general.[1]

Concretely: impersonal definition of rights and duties is one of the distinguishing criteria of bureaucracy. But 'impersonal definition' has meant many things: the rights and duties of the classic Chinese bureaucrat and of an English official in the administrative class are worlds apart, even if both are impersonally defined. Nonetheless, the criterion is indispensable if we are to find all instances of 'bureaucracy' or properly identify those instances we do find. Then we will want to know how general and important the phenomenon of 'impersonal definition' is in a given case. Typically, this involves us in the task of analysing the methods by which the rights and duties of officials are defined, and the degree to which these definitions correspond to behaviour. That analysis will reveal the characteristic discrepancy between formally

1. These and related issues are discussed in Schweitzer (1964). The article will be useful even to those who do not follow all of the author's stimulating suggestions.

stipulated methods and actual implementation, and that discrepancy will raise questions about the utility of the criterion ('impersonal definition') with which we started. Thus the criterion employed simplifies the instances to which it applies, and hence its analytic application poses difficulties. The dilemma is genuine, but there are proximate solutions.

Examination of comparative studies suggests, it seems to me, that definitions of social structures are contrast conceptions. Implicitly or explicitly, we define such terms as feudalism, capitalism, absolutism, caste-system, bureaucracy, and others by contrast with what each of these structures is not. For example, fealty ties are contrasted with contractual ties, absolutist centralized with feudal decentralized authority, caste with tribe or estate, impersonal with personalized administration, the unity of household and business with their separation, etc. My suggestion is that contrast conceptions are indispensable as a first orientation (they serve a function as benchmarks), which introduces analysis, but should not be mistaken for analysis.

Since social structures are defined by several characteristics, more than one contrast conception may be found analytically useful. The choice depends in good measure on the purpose of the inquiry and the historical context. In the emergence of modern bureaucracy, as Weber defined it, the recruitment of officials and their exercise of authority were emancipated from the direct intrusion of kinship relations and property interests. This aspect was in the foreground of attention as long as hereditary privileges prevailed, but has declined in importance along with the rise of egalitarianism in all spheres of modern life. The exclusion of 'every purely personal feeling' remains a valuable desideratum and a proximate characteristic of official conduct, but this condition may not do as much today to ensure administrative impartiality as it did, as long as government by a social elite encouraged the intrusion of family loyalties and property interests upon the conduct of public business. That is, recruitment to official positions on the basis of impersonal criteria and the separation of office and incumbent remain characteristics of bureaucracy, but the changed structure of modern politics has altered their significance. For certain purposes it would be useful, therefore, to formulate an early and a later type of bureaucracy, which would take account of this altered environment of government administration.

F

In this view of the matter, the definition of a social structure in terms of a cluster of traits can serve only as a first approximation. On closer inspection every such trait proves to be an abstraction from the contentions among groups of men. The fealty relation between king and vassal is one of the defining characteristics of feudalism. But the contentions over their reciprocal rights and obligations between these classes of men are resolved in a variety of ways without thereby divesting that relation of the quality of 'fealty'. In this way, social structures are defined by a set of issues which comprise the characteristic areas of contention among the constituent groups of a society. If we then say that one social structure has ceased to exist and another has taken its place, we mean that the terms of reference have changed by which issues are defined, relationships maintained, or contentions resolved. This is the meaning, it seems to me, of Tocqueville's classic specification of the contrast between a feudal and a democratic society.[1]

One corollary of these considerations is that concepts of social structure should be used in two forms. By bureaucracy we mean a depersonalized form of governmental administration, but we know that depersonalization is a matter of degree. Hence we use 'bureaucracy' when we wish to contrast one type of administration with another, and 'bureaucratization' when we wish to emphasize that the new term of reference, e.g. 'depersonalized personnel selection', continues to be problematic, an issue whose every resolution creates new problems as well. Similarly, one can distinguish between democracy and democratization, nation and nation-building, centralized authority and the centralization of authority, etc. Such usage will create linguistic problems from time to time. For example, Max Weber's usage of *Vergesellschaftung* instead of *Gesellschaft* had much the same purpose that I suggest here, but there is no proper English equivalent of this word-form, and it is not exactly usual in German either. Whatever the linguistic difficulties, we should keep the substantive distinction in mind.

By defining social structures in terms of a set of issues, we not only avoid the reification of concepts, but make them 'operational'. If, in this way, we reformulate Max Weber's definition of bureaucracy, we obtain a specification of the issues over which individuals and groups contend in their effort to realize their ideas and maxim-

1. I have used this and other suggestions of the literature in my elaboration of this point in *Nation-building and citizenship* (1964).

ize their chances, however they define these. The consequence of such contentions is a development in the direction of bureaucratization or debureaucratization as the case may be. Analysis of such contentions can account for the changing strength of the 'traits' which characterize a social structure, but are 'never twice the same'.[1]

A third corollary is a reformulation of the concept of equilibrium. Having been taken over from feedback mechanisms such as the thermostat or from biological analysis, the term is widely used by social scientists who employ the concept of 'social system'. Such 'systems' are believed to 'survive' as long as 'they' are in a condition of equilibrium or return to it. The idea has merit in the very general sense that we combine with the concept 'social structure' the notion of some stability and identity over time. We must account for such stability as exists. However, I do not consider the concept 'equilibrium' useful for this purpose, because it is not the social structure or 'the system' that maintains itself in 'equilibrium', whatever that means, but men, who, by their actions (however conditioned), achieve a certain degree of stability, or fail to do so. Here the definition of social structure in terms of a set of issues helps, because it points to the contentions through which individuals and groups achieve a measure of accommodation or compromise between conflicting imperatives.

By way of illustration, I shall reformulate Max Weber's types of domination in keeping with this perspective. The charismatic quality of a personality proves itself by its supernatural attributes (ultimately by miracles), and thereby gains recognition from the ruled. A leader will claim unconditional acceptance of his authority, but, as Weber says, if the test of this claim remains forever wanting, he will appear forsaken by his God or bereft of his heroic powers. Between the leader's unconditional claims and the followers' secret longing for visible signs of his 'gift of grace' this authority relationship will fluctuate one way or another, but it will also

1. I use the example of bureaucracy since, in *Nation-building and citizenship*, pp. 107–15, I have formulated the implications of the general points made here. Similar points are suggested elsewhere in the volume with regard to the contrast between patrimonialism and feudalism, the plebiscitarian and the representative principle in a democracy, the double hierarchy of government in totalitarian régimes, the relation between central and local authority in Indian history. None of these other concepts is as clearly worked out as the concept of bureaucracy.

endure as long as that tension exists. Similarly, under traditional domination, authority is exercised by the ruler in conformity with established precedent. Tradition also confers on him a certain latitude, so that the ruler acts arbitrarily in keeping with tradition. But when he regularly infringes upon the limits set by tradition, he runs the risk of jeopardizing the legitimacy of his own position. Guardians of traditional limits and guardians of the king's prerogatives are, therefore, typical groupings under this type of domination. Finally, Weber distinguishes between formal and substantial rationality of law. The legal order exists as long as neither principle is allowed an absolute ascendance. It is a continuous political and legal task to maintain enough balance between these antagonistic tendencies, for insistence on some principle of material justice can destroy the legal framework just as exaggerated formalism can undermine confidence in the legal system. In this view, stability of a social structure is not an 'equilibrium' that can be attributed to a 'system', but the end-product of always proximate efforts to maintain stability.

Here may be the place also to comment briefly on a problem raised by a German and by an English historian, both of whom warn us against the dangers of substituting inevitably arbitrary categories for the terms in which the historical participants themselves think about the questions at issue.[1] The point is well taken, I believe, and the definition of social structure suggested here allows us to take account of this subjective dimension. But it is also necessary to go beyond that dimension and define the social structure which eventually results from all these contentions, and that cannot be done in subjective terms alone. Indeed, some ab-

---

1. See Brunner, *Neue Wege der Sozialgeschichte* (1956) and Thompson, *The making of the English working class* (1963). In his major work, *Land und Herrschaft* and *Adeliges Landleben und Europäischer Geist*, Brunner reanalyses feudalism in terms of the legal, economic, and ethical categories employed by those directly involved in feudal relationships, but the volume of essays puts this perspective in the larger context of European social history. Thompson, for his part, wishes to restore the meaning of the term 'class' and accordingly he rejects abstract definitions. Class, he says (1963, p. 9), is a historical phenomenon 'which *happens* when some men, as a result of common experiences, feel and articulate the identity of their interests as between themselves and as against other men whose interests are different from theirs'. Note, incidentally, that the same point is made despite the rather marked difference in political orientation of the two authors.

stractions and arbitrariness will be unavoidable in order to 'freeze' the fluidity of historical change for purposes of obtaining benchmarks, as suggested earlier. It may be that the deliberate employment of static *and* dynamic terms, e.g. bureaucracy and bureaucratization, democracy and democratization, etc., provides a way of conceptualizing both the group contentions that are an essential part of change and the altered social structures which from time to time result from that change.

Comparison

The points discussed may now be considered in relation to the comparative analysis of historical change, and specifically of the 'steps and sequences of change in the processes of nation-building and national integration'. Ideally, we should be able to consider all such changes in the same terms, and there is a powerful intellectual legacy which invites us to do so. That legacy goes back to the contrast between tradition and modernity which was first formulated in the romantic period and has been reformulated ever since. Familiar dichotomies such as status and contract, *Gemeinschaft* and *Gesellschaft*, folk and urban society, and others have been given their most systematic formulation in Talcott Parsons's scheme of pattern variables. The utility of these distinctions has been diminished, in my opinion at least, by a tendency toward reification. Nineteenth-century evolutionary theory, for example, imputed to the different aspects of a society 'a strain of consistency with each other, because they all answer their several purposes with less friction and antagonism when they co-operate and support each other' (Sumner, 1940, pp. 5–6). Modern reformulations of this idea in terms of systems-theory and equilibrium are more sophisticated no doubt, and have an impressive array of analogies to draw on, yet they continue to attribute a 'strain of consistency' to social structures such that the 'frictions and antagonisms' between the several traits will diminish – in the famous long run.[1]

On these assumptions it is certainly possible to consider all

1. It is a short step from this thought to a metaphoric language which attributes actions of various kinds to society, the famous fallacy of misplaced concreteness against which Whitehead warned. To me, at least, it has always seemed odd that a theory that began by placing *human* action at the centre of its attention should end up by referring to the actions of *systems*, though that consequence is probably related to the way in which action was defined in the first place.

societies in comparative terms, irrespective of time and space. This approach has been most fully developed with regard to the social and psychological consequences of industrialization, and in the field of national integration with regard to the study of the central value system.

For the scholar interested in comparative studies, the alternative to this approach is to think in terms of concepts applicable to some (rather than all) societies. This strategy of analysis proceeds in the belief that concepts of universals – even if useful for certain orientating purposes – are so emptied of content that they require specifications in order to be applied to some body of evidence and these specifications are concepts of more limited applicability. Examples: interest aggregation is a universal concept, whereas class, estate, political party, etc. are more limited; administration (or should I say goal-attainment?) is universal, but administration by disciples or bureaucrats or patrimonial servants is limited, and so on. By concepts of limited applicability, I mean concepts that are usefully applied to more than one society for a period whose approximate beginning and end are themselves an object of research. Such delimitation is always debatable. But, however difficult in detail, I doubt that it is useful, for example, to speak of class in the absence of a formal legal equality and the freedom of movement and expression that goes with it, or of political parties in the era of politics among cliques of notables, or of the nation-state in the absence of a monopoly of legitimate coercion in the hands of government – although in these and other cases the qualifying criterion is a variable as well as a contrast conception, as discussed earlier. These considerations are equally applicable to 'nation-building'. The concept 'nation' requires delimitation against a period and condition to which it does not apply, and it may be that, with variations in such preconditions, different types of 'nationhood' will have to be formulated. A nation is always in the process of change, for example in the extent to which consensus prevails or different sections of the people have formally equal rights – hence the phrase 'nation-building'.

With regard to this process, the specification of an early and a late condition is necessary, the 'before-and-after' model to which I referred. This is, in fact, a crucial step in the procedure since comparative studies of nation-building depend on the success with which the different dimensions of nation-building can be conceptualized and then compared with one another. In this respect, Stein Rokkan and I have experimented with categories derived from T. H. Marshall's (1950) analysis of *Citizenship and Social Class*, and Karl Deutsch (Deutsch, 1953; Russett & Alker, 1964) has marshalled a great body of evidence on the physical indexes of nation-building.

In some instances it may even be possible to combine quantitative indexes with more qualitative criteria: for example, in the study of the franchise, which has the unique advantage of involving dichotomous choices such as eligibility vs. non-eligibility and voting vs. non-voting. The table below is suggestive in this respect:

EXTENSIONS OF THE FRANCHISE AND CHANGES
IN PARTICIPATION IN PRESIDENTIAL ELECTIONS IN
THE UNITED STATES, FOR SELECTED YEARS

Year	Population (000,000s)	Percentage of population eligible to vote	Percentage of eligible population that voted
1860	27·6	17	84
1880	50·3	23	78
1900	76·1	25	74
1920	106·5	51	49
1940	132·0	61	62
1952	157·0	62	64
1956	168·9	61	60
1960	180·7	60	64

Source: Gendell & Zetterberg (1964, p. 54). The table
is based on figures originally assembled by Lane (1959)
but supplemented for the later years.

With the exception of 1920, the first year adult women had the right to vote throughout the United States, the table gives a graphic picture of the transition from a politics of notables to mass politics under a universal franchise. Voting participation is high as long as voting eligibility exists only for the few, but declines as the franchise is extended. It would be interesting to assemble comparable data for other countries and inquire into the reasons for the differences that would be revealed – a task that would supplement

Almond and Verba's (1963) suggestive study of *Civic Culture* by the addition of a historical dimension. But in what way would it enable us to speak of 'steps and sequences' in the process of nation-building?

In this respect, comparative studies are obliged to develop a typology of nation-building processes before proceeding further, or so it seems to me. This approach is implied in the work of Max Weber and Otto Hintze, whose comparative studies aim at delineating and distinguishing features of the Western European development. In an effort to account for the initial development of capitalism, Weber is concerned with the larger complex of Occidental rationalism, whereas Hintze restricts himself to the relation between social structure and political institutions and seeks to account for the emergence of modern administration and representation. Comparison for both writers means, in the first place, the use of contrasts with other civilizations in order to define more precisely what they wish to explain. Both writers rejected the evolutionism of the nineteenth century not only because they criticized its biological analogies, but because they were interested in developments that were true of more than one society but of less than all.[1]

I want to suggest in what ways I think this perspective to be especially useful for the comparative study of recent historical changes, those broadly suggested by the twin terms of industrialization and democratization. In the introduction to *Capital*, Marx pointed out that he had chosen England as his model because it exemplified the 'laws of capitalist development', which would govern, by and large, the future development of other capitalist countries. Thus he felt that he could say to his German readers: *de te fabula narratur*. This position is, of course, based on the assumption of necessities emanating from the economic structure of societies, which – in the long run – determine political change including international relations. We can now say, I believe, that the facts do not bear this out. Once industrialization had been initiated, no country would go through the same process in similar fashion. Not only were English mechanics used in the early industrialization of Germany, for example, but English institutions were used by German intellectuals as points of reference for the

---

1. Max Weber's critiques of evolutionism are contained in his *Wissenschaftslehre*, Hintze's in several critical essays in *Soziologie und Geschichte*.

development of German institutions. The point is a general one: industrialization itself has intensified the international communication of techniques and ideas, which are taken out of their original context and adopted or adapted to satisfy desires and achieve ends in one's own country. What is here said with reference to the international repercussions of English industrialization applies, *mutatis mutandis*, to the international repercussions of the ideas of the French Revolution.

English industrialization and the French Revolution altered the terms of reference by which 'issues are defined, relationships maintained, and contentions resolved'. Looking backwards from the vantage-point of the eighteenth century, one is justified in emphasizing the continuity of the changes in Western Europe which culminated in these events, and which Weber and Hintze analysed as distinguishing characteristics of Occidental civilization. That industrialization and democratization emerged from a long and distinctly European development may help to account for the strong tendency of social scientists to consider change a phenomenon that is internal to the societies changing. It is equally legitimate to regard industrialization and democratization as having been 'initiated' at a particular time and place and as constituting a 'breakthrough' to a new historical era. If one considers the great transformations that followed, one is inclined to highlight the contrast between pre-revolutionary traditions and post-revolutionary modernity. This contrast has been a dominant theme of social theory from the eighteenth century to the present, and it underlies many of the generalizations that have been derived from the Western experience. However, these same perspectives may be used in a different manner. Emphasis may be placed on the persistent distinctiveness of the Western experience which is as notable in its feudal traditions as in its modern industrialism and democracy. Although long in the making in Western Europe as a whole, the twin revolutions of the eighteenth century came to a head in England and France, and since then this impetus to change has had repercussions in other Western European countries and in European settlements overseas. These repercussions may be considered an extension of the internal continuities of the pre-revolutionary development analysed by Weber and Hintze.

Let me try to characterize these repercussions by restructuring what we know about certain pervasive differences between intellectual and working-class alienation and agitation during the nineteenth century. The alienation of intellectuals is a by-product of industrialization itself, for industrialization creates a mass public and a market for intellectual products and thus accentuates the elitism of some, the populism of others, and the ambivalence of all intellectuals, especially through their awareness of the discrepancies between high culture and popular culture. This general alienation was overshadowed as well as greatly intensified in the countries that witnessed from afar the rapid economic advance of England and the stirring events of the French Revolution, so that their own economic backwardness and autocratic institutions appeared still more backward and autocratic by comparison. Under these conditions a polarization of cultural life has typically occurred between those who would see their own country progress by imitating the 'more advanced countries' and those who denounce that advance as alien and evil and emphasize instead the wellsprings of strength that exist among the people and within the native culture. This reaction was typified by the difference between Westernizers and Slavophils in Tsarist Russia; recently its convolutions have been analysed with great subtlety by Levenson in his work *Confucian China and its Modern Fate* (1958). The general pattern has occurred again and again; it has been a mainspring not only of intellectual alienation but also of movements for national independence where these have occurred.

Working-class alienation and agitation during the nineteenth century involved very different processes, as I have argued in *Nation-Building and Citizenship* (1964). Intellectuals could experience industrialization as an emancipation from their previous subservience to the Church and to private patrons. But workers experienced it initially as economic destitution exacerbated by legal and political changes which – under the slogan of individual freedom – made a mockery of their position as members of the community. For workers, alienation meant simply second-class citizenship reinforced by police measures and the ideological indignities heaped upon them through sermons and public debates. As a result, radical agitation among workers represented a protest against this type of discrimination, a point largely obscured by Marx, whose theory of alienation attributes to workers types of dissatisfaction more often found among intellectuals. There is a strong civic component in much working-class agitation that is missing from the radical agitation of intellectuals, since their citizenship was never in question. And, conversely: the alienation of intellectuals also occurs in countries like the United States in which workers have a strong sense of citizenship and reject radical appeals. However, the two kinds of movement have joined in various blends of socialism and nationalism, where the workers' protest against second-class citizenship and the intellectuals' ambivalence about the comparative backwardness of their country and their own role in it are not sufficiently assuaged.

In Europe these nineteenth-century movements occurred in the context of an emerging nation-state. They were preceded by developments which furthered an absolutist concentration of power, on the one hand, and a more or less individualized citizenry, on the other. At the risk of putting a very complex matter too simply, I would say that the desire of the workers for full citizenship and the search of the intellectuals for a power capable of removing the backwardness of their country had a common precondition in the prior decline of kinship ties, religious belief, linguistic affiliation, and territorial and racial communalism. None of these ties or associations disappeared, but some of them had been weakened by the ascendance of Christianity, others by the Renaissance and the Reformation, and others still in the course of struggles between enlightened absolutism and the estates. It will be recalled that Max Weber's lifework documents the proposition that Christian doctrine and the revival of Roman law militated against familial and communal ties as foci of loyalty that could compete effectively with the universal claims of legal procedure and the Christian faith. By these prior developments men were freed very gradually for such alternative solidarities as those of social class and national citizenship, though the relative decline of 'traditional' and the relative ascendance of 'modern' solidarities remains an issue to this day and hence a major subject of comparative study in Europe as well.

Here is the place, it seems to me, to refer to that loss of community which has been a recurrent theme of social theory ever since the eighteenth century. The reference can be made without nostalgia or false romanticism, if it is accompanied by an appreciation of these alternative solidarities, and hence by a proper balancing of the assets and liabilities of such a development.

The 'new nations' of today are in a fundamentally different

position from the 'new nations' of Western Europe during the nineteenth century. Indeed, the applicability of the term 'nation' itself is in question. The long European pre-history, in the course of which familial and communal ties gradually weakened, is notably absent from the societies which have gained their independence since World War II.[1] In these societies industrialization has become an almost universal ambition, and the populism of the franchise (if not democracy) an equally universal reality – in good part as a reaction against Western colonialism but still also as a result of influences emanating from Europe. One effect of the right to vote has been that just those familial and communal ties are mobilized politically that militate against the emergence of civic loyalties, and hence against at least one of the preconditions of the nation-state that are familiar to us from the Western experience. The consequence of this new historical pattern may be as great eventually as the consequences of the twin revolutions in eighteenth-century Europe. At any rate, there is no precedent in our experience for the emergence of 'nations' in the context of three competing world systems which can quickly transform every tension of a social structure into an issue of international relations under the threat of nuclear war.

REFERENCES

ALMOND, G. A. & COLEMAN, J. S. (eds.) (1960) *The politics of the developing areas*. Princeton, N.J.: Princeton University Press.

ALMOND, G. A. & VERBA, S. (1963) *The civic culture: political attitudes and democracy in five nations*. Princeton, N.J.: Princeton University Press.

BELLAH, R. N. (1964) Religious evolution. *Amer. sociol. Rev.* **29**, 358–74.

BENDIX, REINHARD (1964) *Nation-building and citizenship*. New York: Wiley.

1. That, it seems to me, is the questionable part of Lipset's analysis in *The first new nation* (1963), since the achievement of political independence at the end of the eighteenth century is comparable with a similar achievement in the middle of the twentieth century only on the assumption that all achievements of independence by former colonies are comparable – irrespective of time and place. I do not consider the utility of that assumption very great, but whatever it may be it is diminished, it seems to me, by the neglect of the obvious differences between independence movements then and now.

BRUNNER, OTTO (1949) *Adeliges Landleben und Europ ischer Geist.* Salzburg: Otto Müller Verlag.

BRUNNER, OTTO (1956) *Neue Wege der Sozialgeschichte.* Göttingen: Vandenhoeck & Ruprecht.

BRUNNER, OTTO (1959) *Land und Herrschaft.* Wien: Rudolf M. Rohrer Verlag.

DEUTSCH, KARL (1953) *Nationalism and social communication.* New York: Wiley.

EISENSTADT, S. N. (1964) Social change, differentiation and evolution. *Amer. sociol. Rev.* **29**, 375–86.

GENDELL, MURRAY & ZETTERBERG, HANS L. (1964) *A sociological almanac for the United States.* New York: Charles Scribner's Sons.

GOTTSCHALK, LOUIS (ed.) (1963) *Generalizations in the writing of history.* Chicago: Chicago University Press.

HINTZE, OTTO (1964) *Soziologie und Geschichte.* 2nd edn. Göttingen: Vandenhoeck & Ruprecht.

LANE, R. E. (1959) *Political life: why people get involved in politics.* Glencoe, Ill.: Free Press.

LERNER, DANIEL (1965) Comparative analysis of processes of modernization. Paper submitted to International Social Science Council Round Table on Comparative Research, Paris, 22–24 April. (Unpublished.)

LEVENSON, J. R. (1958) *Confucian China and its modern fate.* Vol. I, *The problem of intellectual continuity.* Berkeley: University of California Press; London: Routledge & Kegan Paul.

LIPSET, S. M. (1963) *The first new nation: the United States in historical and comparative perspective.* New York: Basic Books.

MARSHALL, T. H. (1950) *Citizenship and social class.* London: Cambridge University Press.

MERTON, ROBERT K. (1957) *Social theory and social structure.* (2nd rev. edn.) Glencoe, Ill.: Free Press.

PARSONS, TALCOTT (1964) Evolutionary universals in society. *Amer. sociol. Rev.* **29,** 339–57.

RUSSETT, BRUCE M., ALKER, HAYWARD, R., et al. (1964) *World handbook of political and social indicators.* New Haven, Conn.: Yale University Press.

SCHWEITZER, ARTHUR (1964) Vom Idealtypus zum Prototyp. *Z. ges. Staatswiss.* **120,** 13–55.

SNELL, BRUNO (1964) *Scenes from Greek drama.* Berkeley: University of California Press.

SOCIAL SCIENCE RESEARCH COUNCIL (1946) *Theory and practice in historical study: a report of the Committee on Historiography.* New York: Social Science Research Council Bulletin 54.

SOCIAL SCIENCE RESEARCH COUNCIL (1954) *The social sciences in historical study: a report of the Committee on Historiography.* Social Science Research Council Bulletin 64.

SUMNER, W. G. (1940) *Folkways.* Boston: Ginn.

THOMPSON, E. P. (1963) *The making of the English working class.* London: Gollancz; New York: Pantheon, 1964.

WATT, I. & GOODY, J. (1963) The consequences of literacy. *Comp. Stud. Soc. Hist.* **5**, 304–45.

WEBER, MAX (1922) *Gesammelte Aufsätze zur Wissenschaftslehre.* Tübingen: J. C. B. Mohr (Paul Siebeck).

The Social Psychology of
Social Change

MICHAEL ARGYLE

Large-scale changes in society, such as the Industrial Revolution, consist ultimately of changes in the behaviour of a large number of individuals, and are initiated by the behaviour of a smaller number of other individuals. In principle, therefore, social psychology should be able to throw some light on what happens. Most research in social psychology has, however, been carried out in much more limited social settings. In this paper we shall consider research into the social psychological basis of social change in three settings which have been extensively studied – small social groups, social organizations, and the spread of ideologies in the community. We shall see that certain common principles about the basis of social change will emerge, and we shall then consider how far these principles can illuminate wider social changes. In this connexion we shall examine theories such as Hagen's and McClelland's about the origins of social change, and see what use can be made of empirical evidence about national character and patterns of child-rearing. This is an unfamiliar type of data for social historians, and the evidence of social psychology may seem rather remote from the phenomena of historical change. Nevertheless, there is a great deal of carefully collected empirical evidence concerning the more limited types of change that we shall consider, and it is hoped that some light may be thrown on the processes of social interaction involved in other kinds of social change.

Change in Small Social Groups

Small social groups always develop 'norms', i.e. shared ways of behaving, thinking, and feeling, especially in relation to the main goals and activities of the group. These can be thought of as constituting the culture-pattern of the group at a given time. The norms can be changed through the action of one or more individual members of the group. Under what conditions is this likely to happen?

In the first place, it depends on the state of the group. The group norms exert a kind of conservative influence, resisting change, so that there is always a tendency for the norms to become out of date as a result of changes in the environment outside the group. The norms will no longer prescribe ways of behaving which success-fully meet the needs of the members, and a discontented minority may be created which is particularly dissatisfied with the way things are done. Sometimes, outside events produce a state of crisis in the group, when previous patterns of behaviour suddenly become quite useless. This situation was created experimentally by Hamblin (1958): groups of three played a series of games and grad-ually learnt the rules; suddenly, the rules were changed by the experi-menter. It was found that the previously most influential leaders became more influential during the crisis, though some groups replaced their leader if he did not deal quickly with the crisis.

Whether or not an individual will try to bring about a change in a group depends on his motivation. If he is a member of a dis-contented minority he may attempt either to change the group or to form a break-away splinter group, depending on the strength of his attachment to the group. Members will be more concerned about the group's activities if their own needs are closely linked with the group's goals. For example, a person may have a great need for money, and be a member of an industrial work-group which is paid on group piece-work. Similarly, a member of a team may have a great desire for fame or success, and this may be dependent on the success of the team. Whether or not a member wants to influence the group also depends on the balance of his various social motivations. Statistical analyses of social interaction show that it can be classified in terms of two main dimensions, as in the figure below (Foa, 1961). A person whose dominance

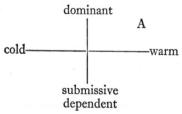

needs are strong will seek to exert influence and give orders, whereas a person whose affiliative needs are strong will want to make friends with the other members rather than influence them. In some studies it has been found that there are two kinds of leader – a task leader who takes decisions and a socio-emotional leader who keeps people happy.

A person may want to influence the group, but he will not be able to do so unless he is acceptable to the group. At one time it was thought that there was a kind of person who was a natural leader, but now it is realized that a person who leads in one group may have no influence at all in another. In fact, there is a small statistical tendency for greater influence to be exerted by those who are intelligent, extraverted, well adjusted, socially sensitive, and of high status outside the group. More important, however, is the contribution a person can make to the group – in helping it to attain its goals. It has been shown in experiments in which groups are given different tasks to do that the person who is best at or knows most about each task tends to become the leader (Argyle 1957, p. 137f). Similarly, it is found in delinquent gangs that the boys who lead in the sphere of criminal activity are quite different from those who lead in football.

A problem about the initiation of change in groups is that any-one who deviates from the norms is liable to be rejected: how, then, is influence ever exerted? This problem is dealt with by Hollander (1964) in his theory of 'idiosyncrasy credit'. According to this theory, members accumulate such credit – a kind of licence to deviate – on the strength of valuable contributions they have made in the past. This is partly because their deviating suggestions will be seen as useful ideas rather than as irresponsible failures to keep up with group standards. Another way of looking at the leadership of small social groups is as an exchange of gifts (Homans, 1961): the group will allow a member to have influence only if he provides sufficient gratifications for them. This approach can be illustrated in terms of the dimensions shown in the figure opposite. The effective leader should operate in Sector A. In fact, it is very hard to do this, because if the leader is too dominant the group is resentful and the affiliative bond is broken, and if he becomes too friendly he loses his authority. The solution probably lies in a rather subtle style of behaviour, which has been found to be the most effective kind of leadership in face-to-face groups. The leader exerts influence,

G

but in a persuasive and consultative way; he resists the influence of the group; and he is highly rewarding to the group. To avoid being influenced by the group the leader may require some degree of detachment or aloofness, some studies suggest.

A member may be personally acceptable as a source of influence but his ideas also need to be acceptable to the group. They will be acceptable if they really are to the advantage of the members, or can be made to appear so. It is here that the skills of persuasion come in, and we shall discuss these later in connexion with the spread of ideologies. Although a leader can rely to some extent on his idiosyncrasy credit and put forward ideas that depart from the previous group norms, he will be more successful if his plans do not deviate too far and if they are consistent with the general values and goals of the group.

The Spread of Ideologies

We shall consider, next, the spread of ideologies, since the factors to be taken into account are largely similar to those discussed above in relation to change in small social groups, whereas change in social organizations requires the introduction of some quite new concepts. By ideologies we mean not only political and religious beliefs and attitudes, but also ideas about commercial products, for example, or about how to rear children, and attitudes towards members of other racial and national groups. Persuading large numbers of people involves different techniques from persuading the members of a small group. It is usually done by means of public meetings, and via the mass media of communication – TV, radio, pamphlets, and posters.

Change will be more likely if the people in the community are in a state of deprivation or conflict, causing them anxiety or distress. A leader or group who appears to be able to solve their problems will attract followers. For instance, Protestant sects have spread in many lands because they have appealed in various ways to the underprivileged (Argyle, 1958). New ideas may also appeal to the uprooted and the anomic, because such people have no group norms to oppose them and because the new movement provides them with something to belong to.

Why does a person want to propagate his ideas? In the first place, he is unlikely to want to do so unless his own beliefs are very strongly held, and this usually means that they meet some very strong personal need. For example, an aggressive person might believe that corporal punishment was a good thing; a person with anxiety about aggression would not take this view. An ideological leader has usually shared the tensions and conflicts that are common in his community, and the new ideas constitute his psychological resolution of the problems that gave rise to them. To arrive at such new ideas requires 'creativity'. A certain amount is known about the psychological basis of creative people: they are open to new rather than stereotyped solutions to problems; they prefer complex and irregular patterns; they enjoy intellectual problems; in social behaviour they are independent and unconventional (Barron, 1957). Social reformers and political leaders, on the other hand, have often become sensitized to particular social problems and to the troubles of particular groups.

What kind of person with new ideas is likely to be successful in putting them across? He must not be a person who is very dependent on affiliative satisfactions, or he is likely to submit to pressures to conform. Similarly, he must not be authoritarian, or he will submit to pressures from people in authority; in any case, authoritarians do not arrive at original solutions to problems. It is curious that many successful ideological leaders have shown symptoms of mental disorder, especially in the case of religious innovators. L. C. Hauesser is one example of a person who was, at different times, diagnosed as psychotic and accepted as a leader by many followers (Argyle, 1958, p. 109f). However, such leaders differ from mental patients proper in at least two important respects. First, the problems with which they are concerned are universal problems rather than purely private ones. Second, the successful leader is able to organize and lead a social movement, whereas the mental patient cannot even organize his own life. A leader will carry more weight if he has prestige, and the possession of symptoms of schizophrenia or hysteria may actually convey religious prestige in some times and places. It would not, on the other hand, carry much weight in a senior civil servant. Prestige can be won by actual past achievements, or it can be built up by a skilful public relations campaign. It can also be established by a speaker at a public meeting through subtle indications of his competence, sincerity, good intentions, reliable views, membership of the group, and so on. An ideological leader requires certain special social skills, which are rather different from those needed in a primary group leader. He must be able to handle public meetings, and generate emotional arousal at them. Hysterics are selected as priests in some African sects because of their ability to work themselves up into a state of 'possession'. An ideological leader must be able to attract and keep the loyalty of followers. And he must be able to organize the movement, and deal with a changing situation outside. As the movement gathers force and the leader becomes to some extent recognized as a leader, he will undergo a change in ego-identity: he will see himself in the role of leader or prophet, and this will give him a further incentive to propagate his ideas.

What sort of new ideas will be acceptable? We have really answered this question already – they will be ideas that help to solve widespread psychological problems. For example, the Townsend plan in America was an economically unsound scheme for providing old-age pensions. Economists may not have supported it, but many thousands of old people did (Cantril, 1941). Again, despite the spread of education in Ghana, there has been a considerable increase in pagan shrines. The reason is that economic stresses have led to an increased fear of witchcraft and the shrines offer protection against witchcraft.

Change in Social Organizations

When we consider change in social organizations, such as industrial firms, hospitals, prisons, and the like, there are additional factors to be taken into account. The methods whereby change is brought about usually include those already mentioned, i.e. the influencing of face-to-face groups and the use of public meetings and the mass media. In addition, the senior members of organizations have the power to issue directions to junior personnel, though it may be more difficult to get these actually carried out. Furthermore, administrative techniques can be used to bring about changes in organizations. One is the introduction of new lines of communication, by setting up joint consultative committees, for instance. A second is the devising of training courses, in which members may be introduced to new ideas and new ways of working. Third, it is possible to control the selection of new personnel so that only certain types of people are admitted.

When will an organization be ready for change? One condition echoes what we said about small social groups – change is most likely when there is widespread dissatisfaction. Whether or not this will stimulate change depends on how clearly the voices of those at the bottom of the organization can be heard by those at the top. Obviously in prisons and other 'total institutions', where there is a sharp social division between the inmates and the staff, the latter are not likely to be very worried about the welfare of the former (Goffman, 1957). In industrial undertakings or the armed services, on the other hand, discontent lower down will be re-flected in labour turnover and absenteeism, and in the general inefficiency of the organization. This brings us to the second condition – an organization will be ready for change when it becomes clear that it is ineffective in the attainment of its stated goals. A factory may have low output, a prison a high rate of recidivism, an army may lose its battles. All those who have any measure of responsibility and decision-making, if they realize the state of affairs, will demand changes to increase organizational effectiveness. However, they may not perceive that the organiza-tion is ineffective, and they may not know the remedy, unless experts in the form of consultants, industrial psychologists, or others give them the necessary information. Thus the ultimate source of organizational change is likely to be a social scientist or other expert. But the actual implementation of the change must be done by the senior administrators of the organization.

One type of organizational change, which has been very wide-spread in industry, derives from the so-called human relations movement. It originated partly in a number of studies by industrial social psychologists which showed that output is higher when supervisors are democratic and employee-centred. Recent re-search has found that a stricter style of supervision is more effective when the job requires meticulous timing and accuracy (Fiedler, 1964). A democratic style of supervision can be brought about in three ways – by the selection and training of supervisors, and by the example of senior managers. A second kind of change which has been induced by research and consultants is the redesign of work-flow systems so that they function better from the human point of view. Much of the work of the Tavistock Institute is relevant in this connexion. Work-flow systems may unintentionally produce conflicts between people who need to co-operate, or pre-vent communication between people who need to communicate. Imaginative redesigning of the work-flow can correct these faults on the human side. Another type of industrial change aims to make work more interesting and satisfying. 'Job enlargement' is a partial reversal of the rationalization of work by work-study engineers: workers carry out a greater variety of activities, and are able to complete a more meaningful task. Some of these changes can be shown to work only by actual experimentation in the field situation. The parallel trend towards therapeutic communities in mental hospitals and prisons was started by research-minded administrators of such organizations.

What will motivate an administrator to bring about organizational changes? At the highest level he will be concerned about the efficiency of the organization – the goals of the organization have become *his* goals. At the next level he may want to bring about changes that will strengthen his position, or his part of the organization. At a lower level he may want to present an appearance of keenness and efficiency to impress his superiors and secure his eventual promotion.

What kind of person will succeed in bringing about changes in an organization? Ability to persuade individuals and committees is important, but in this setting new features appear. First, the individual should possess formal power, that is, he should be in a position to sanction rewards and punishments for other people, and to this extent be able to control their behaviour. Second, people in organizations are more successful if they possess what can loosely be described as political or organizational skill. This may involve getting other influential people on their side through offering bargains, establishing committees or lines of communication, controlling selection and training, and so forth.

Certain styles of administration are more successful than others. The main principle here is that subordinates should be persuaded and motivated rather than ordered – so that they actually want to behave in the new way. This persuasive and democratic style means allowing people to take part in discussion and decisions. A number of field experiments demonstrate the superior effectiveness of this approach (Argyle, 1957, p. 197f). Unfortunately, the more highly technical the activities of the organization, the less possible it is for the junior ranks to participate fully in these ways, though they can still have a say in the details of pay, training, and conditions of work.

What sort of changes will be acceptable in an organization?

In the first place, there is usually resistance to change of any sort. Small groups are resistant to change because their norms lead to the rejection of deviates. In social organizations, patterns of behaviour become established and are of great stability because individuals work out drive-reducing ways of adapting, and fear that any change will be to their disadvantage in some way. Changes in industry are resisted by workers because they are afraid that they will be paid less or will have to work harder to earn the same amount. Wage-incentive schemes have often foundered for this reason. Changes are resisted by managers because they are afraid that their position will be weakened somehow or that they will be further from the centre of power. Current changes in prisons are resisted by prison officers and prisoners alike because they have no desire to associate with each other (McCleery, 1957). There is anxiety either about possible material loss or about the disruption of a well-established and satisfying social system. It may be impossible to bring about change in the teeth of such resistance, and it is usually possible only if the new scheme can be shown to be advantageous. This may be achieved by means of financial incentives, honorific ranks, training courses, or by sheer persuasive skill.

Wider Social and Economic Changes

We turn now to social changes at the level of society as a whole – the Industrial Revolution, changes in the class system, changes in the family, and so on. Can analysis at the level of social psychology be applied to events on this scale? We have now looked at the phenomenon of social change in three more limited contexts where it has been studied by the techniques of social psychology. It seems probable that variables not unlike those that were relevant in these settings will also be involved in respect of society as a whole. There is not much social psychological evidence about social change on this scale, but there is a certain amount of pertinent information.

Under what conditions will a society be ready for major social changes? Personal discontent usually becomes channelled into political parties, which may become the means of change. Internal conflicts and stress may lead to religious or other ideological movements. Dissatisfaction with the state of the nation can be a major element in social change, particularly since the mass media now communicate such ideas so rapidly. The reform of American schools was hastened by the Sputnik, the rise of Nazism by anger at national humiliation.

It has been suggested that the national character will make certain developments more probable. McClelland (1961) collected children's stories which were popular in 1925 from forty different countries, and scored them for the presence of achievement themes. It was assumed that preference for achievement stories would indicate the presence of achievement motivation in the young readers. A correlation of ·46 was found between these achievement scores and economic growth in the countries concerned during the next twenty-five years. This is an impressive finding, though it does not necessarily show that achievement motivation in the national character *causes* economic growth. It could be that, when economic growth is in the air, children tend to be trained in a way that emphasizes achievement – just as warlike tribes train their children to be aggressive. There are also doubts about the validity of this method of measuring achievement motivation: laboratory experiments have not found a very consistent relationship between projective measures of achievement and achievement-oriented behaviour. However, McClelland's cross-cultural findings can be defended on the ground that the measure of achievement motivation referred to a period *before* the economic growth occurred. A more serious point, perhaps, is that achievement motivation may seek a variety of outlets: making money and expanding business may be the characteristic American version of it, but in other times and places it may lead to very different kinds of achievement. It is this consideration that throws some doubt on McClelland's deduction that the way to help underdeveloped countries is to send out experts on child-rearing who would persuade the parents to inculcate greater achievement motivation in their children. The result might be that the people built bigger canoes, cast stronger spells, or jumped from taller trees, rather than that they set up factories and power stations. This is not to say that changing the national character would not be useful, but other things may need to be done too. It has been observed in some underdeveloped countries that when it becomes possible to make money people will work very hard to do this. There are often cultural barriers to the accumulation of capital – fear of witchcraft on the part of envious people, and the tradition of sharing property with large numbers of distant relatives – but, even so, capitalists will emerge (Herskovits, 1962).

We have stressed achievement motivation here because it is important for economic development. However, motivation of many kinds may provide the roots for social change. Another interesting finding of McClelland's study was that those countries in which the children were high in power motivation in 1925 have dictatorships or authoritarian régimes today.

How far is the national character affected by the way in which children are brought up by their parents? This would be valuable information for historians if they could find evidence about methods of child-rearing. What we mean here by 'national character' is the typical or common type of personality in a society, or part of a society; i.e. how aggressive, achievement-oriented, neurotic, extraverted, and so on, people are. All these states are partly inherited, as numerous twin studies show, but the impact of environmental experiences is greater. And the most significant experiences occur in the family, though not necessarily in the very early years, as some psychologists have suggested. The actual ways in which parental behaviour affects the personalities of their children are very complex, and discussion of them is beyond the scope of this paper (see Argyle, 1964). The origins of achievement motivation, for example, are at least threefold. First, such motivation is dependent on certain types of reward – emotional rewards for success, as well as the actual experience of success. Second, it is brought about through a relation of identification with the parents, when they are themselves achievement-oriented. Third, it can result from the parents' exhorting to greater efforts and setting high standards; this makes people feel that they 'ought' to work hard, as opposed to 'wanting' to work hard (Argyle & Robinson, 1962).

If child-rearing causes personality, what causes child-rearing? It is partly a matter of a tradition passed on to mothers, but it is a tradition that can change quite rapidly, as the comparison of successive American studies shows (Bronfenbrenner, 1958). The sources of change include widely read baby books, like that of Spock, and other channels of advice to mothers. There is some evidence that fashions in child-rearing start in the middle class and filter through to the working class. There are fairly wide variations in a given society, largely due to the personalities of the parents –

for example, aggressive parents beat their children more, as do mothers who are discontented in this role. It is quite conceivable that major social changes could be brought about through persuading parents to change their style of child-rearing.

In what ways could social and economic historians make use of information about national character or child-rearing? Certainly the relevant information does not at first sight appear to be readily available, but it has been said that as soon as historians feel the need for a certain type of information they quickly discover ways of getting it. Contemporary and recent data on child-rearing are available for a number of societies. Only in America have these studies been conducted over a sufficiently long period for changes in child-rearing to be seen (Bronfenbrenner, 1958). Certain aspects of parent behaviour could be studied fairly easily – such as family size, absence of fathers, roles of servants, and so on. There are accounts of how children were reared in Victorian England and other periods, which should be a usable source of data. Unfortunately, such accounts tend to be restricted to the more literate sections of society, and material on the others may be more difficult to get. Information about national character may also prove difficult to obtain. As a matter of fact, it is extremely hard to get reliable data on this topic even in the present, let alone the past. Strictly speaking, what is needed is the testing of representative samples of different populations, by means of tests that are cross-culturally valid. This has never been done. The nearest we can get to it is to compare the findings of social surveys, using identical questions in different countries. Another approach is to compare smaller numbers of equivalent groups, such as students, in various experimental situations. With this method it was found that Norwegian students were more conformist than French in a social pressure situation (Milgram, 1961). It is not clear what sort of historical evidence might serve as an index of national character in the past. McClelland (1961) made use of imaginative productions for this purpose. He applied a method of scoring pictures to assess Greek vases for the presence of achievement motivation. He found that the latter was strongest during the period of expansion of the Greek empire, weakest during its decline. It should also be possible to make reasonably valid inferences about national character from features of the popular culture – whether people choose to spend their spare time watching bear-baiting, or in love-making, competitive games, or prayer and fasting, for example.

Having considered the conditions under which a society will be ready for social change, we turn to the people who initiate such change. These are of a number of types, and include ideological leaders (as discussed above), political leaders (who are similar to the administrators in charge of organizations), and experts and inventors who discover new ways of doing things. The latter are not 'leaders' in the usual sense, and it is necessary for others to promote their inventions. What motivates a person who induces changes in society? As in the three simpler cases discussed earlier, he may be seeking his own advantage in one way or another. He may, for example, be trying to make money through business enterprises. There is no doubt that the pursuit of wealth is extremely important here as elsewhere in human behaviour. The objection to the doctrine of economic man is simply that people are motivated in other ways too, so that in many circumstances they do not take the most profitable path. They may be more interested in fame, glory, or public recognition. They may become concerned for the fate or success of the country, community, or organization – and this is especially likely in the case of a person who is one of the leaders. They may become interested in the welfare of some under-privileged group, or have ideas about how society *should* be arranged. Social scientists have become sensitized through their research to a number of social problems and have played a primary part in getting something done – about the poor, prison-ers, mental patients, industrial workers, and others. Again, an innovator may care nothing about any of these things but be curious about a particular field of science, technology, or gadgetry, and arrive at discoveries or inventions which have totally unfore-seen consequences.

Hagen (1962) has suggested another motivation for the origi-nators of social change. He maintains that, when a social group has declined in social status, the sons of a later generation, spurred on by their mothers, may become technological innovators. While this goes against the finding that achievement needs are commonly based on identification with the *same*-sex parent, there is some evidence that upwardly mobile working-class students in England often have very ambitious mothers. The theory does not explain why *technological* innovation should be selected, nor is the evidence very convincing that a family history of status deprivation in

previous generations is significant. Among the educated and potentially influential members of a society there are many not of the
highest social status, so that the probability is that a successful
innovator will not come from the very top.

What kind of person will be most acceptable as a source of new
ideas. The possession of formal power and of prestige is useful.
This can be added to either by real accomplishments or by means
of public relations. Some people are influential through being
'opinion leaders', i.e. they are at the centre of the web of informal
contacts along which ideas and advice flow. Or they may have
access to the mass media, which can be achieved in a number of
ways, including being able to pay for it. They should possess other
social skills of several kinds, such as the ability to persuade
individuals, to handle small groups and public meetings, and to
run social organizations; sensitivity to the needs of people in the
community is also valuable. Such skills have been systematized
and professionalized in the motivation research techniques used
in the promotion of commercial products and political parties.

What kinds of social change will be most acceptable? As before,
the general answer is that ideas are acceptable which appeal to
widespread needs of some kind. Effective market research can
discover what these are, and the product may then be sold to large
numbers of people. As with organizations, there will be resistance
to change, but this can be overcome by techniques of governmental
control, including laws, taxes, and duties, and by government
grants – to encourage child-bearing, education, or other objectives
thought desirable. Social control can be exercised in a number of
ways – through the mass media, for example, or by means of the
education system or selection policies.

By considering psychological research in more limited areas of
social change we have been able to outline some of the main variables that need to be taken into account in the analysis of historical
change. We have noted the influence of widespread conditions of
deprivation or stress, and the role of leaders who possess qualities
of creativity and social skill, and whose ideas meet the needs of the
community. If historians could manage to collect the necessary
kinds of data – about child-rearing, national character, and the
personalities of innovators – they would be able to add consider-
ably to the understanding of historical processes. The rate of social
change has increased very rapidly during the twentieth century,

partly owing to the development of new vehicles for social change, such as the mass media and new governmental controls. Reliable social psychological data could contribute to the analysis and understanding of these processes.

REFERENCES

ARGYLE, M. (1957) *The scientific study of social behaviour*. London: Methuen.

ARGYLE, M. (1958) *Religious behaviour*. London: Routledge & Kegan Paul.

ARGYLE, M. (1964) *Psychology and social problems*. London: Methuen.

ARGYLE, M. & ROBINSON, P. (1962) Two origins of achievement motivation. *Brit. J. soc. clin. Psychol.* **1**, 107–20.

BARRON, F. (1957) Originality in relation to personality and intellect. *J. Pers.* **25**, 730–42.

BRONFENBRENNER, U. (1958) Socialization and social class through time and space. In E. E. Maccoby, T. M. Newcomb & H. Hartley (eds.), *Readings in social psychology*. New York: Holt.

CANTRIL, H. (1941) *The psychology of social movements*. London: Chapman & Hall.

FIEDLER, F. E. (1964) A contingency model of leadership effectiveness. In L. Berkowitz (ed.), *Advances in experimental social psychology*, Vol. 1. New York: Academic Press.

FOA, U. G. (1961) Convergences in the analysis of the structure of interpersonal behaviour. *Psychol. Rev.* **68**, 341–53.

GOFFMAN, E. (1957) Characteristics of total institutions. In M. R. Stein *et al.* (eds.), *Identity and anxiety*. Glencoe, Ill.: Free Press.

HAGEN, E. E. (1962) *On the theory of social change*. Homewood, Ill.: Dorsey Press; London: Tavistock Publications, 1964.

HAMBLIN, R. L. (1958) Leadership and crisis. *Sociometry* **21**, 322–35.

HERSKOVITS, M. J. (1962) *Human problems in changing Africa*. New York: Knopf.

HOMANS, G. C. (1961) *Social behavior: its elementary forms*. New York: Harcourt Brace

HOLLANDER, E. P. (1964) *Leaders, groups and influence*. New York: Oxford University Press.

MCCLELLAND, D. C. (1961) *The achieving society*. Princeton, N. J. Van. Nostrand.

MCCLEERY, R. H. (1957) *Policy change in prison management*. Governmental Research Bureau, Michigan State University.

MILGRAM, S. (1961) Nationality and conformity. *Sci. Amer.* **205**, 45–51.

Biographical Notes

MICHAEL ARGYLE is University Lecturer in Social Psychology at Oxford and a Fellow of Wolfson College. After serving as a navigator in the RAF, he read Moral Sciences and Experimental Psychology at Cambridge, coming to Oxford in 1952. He was a Fellow at the Center for Advanced Study in the Behavioral Sciences, Stanford, and has been visiting lecturer or professor at the Universities of Michigan, British Columbia, Ghana, and Delaware. He is at present joint editor of the *British Journal of Social and Clinical Psychology* and Chairman of the Social Psychology Section of the British Psychological Society. He is author of *The scientific study of social behaviour* (1957), *Religious behaviour* (1958), *Psychology and social problems* (1964), and *The psychology of interpersonal behaviour* (1967), and of numerous papers in British and American journals. He is director of the Oxford Social Skills research group.

REINHARD BENDIX, M.A., Ph.D., is Professor of Sociology at the University of California, Berkeley. He obtained his academic degrees at the University of Chicago, where he became Instructor in the Social Science Division, and was subsequently appointed Assistant Professor of Sociology at the University of Colorado. He joined the staff of the University of California in 1947. In 1964–65 he was Theodor Heuss Professor at the Free University of Berlin, and in 1965–66 was Visiting Fellow at St Catherine's College, Oxford. He has been Vice-President of the American Sociological Association and a member of the Advisory Council to the Pacific Sociological Association. In 1966 he was elected Vice-President of the International Sociological Association.

Professor Bendix is the author of numerous books and papers. His current research interests are in comparative developmental studies, with special emphasis on changes in social stratification.

TOM BURNS is Professor of Sociology at the University of Edinburgh. He is the author of *Local government & central control, The management of innovation* (with G. M. Stalker), and a number of other publications on industrial and non-industrial organizations. His current interests are in international studies of organization and industrialism in general and in the sociology of consumer behaviour.

M. W. Flinn, M.A., D.Litt., is Reader in Economic History at the University of Edinburgh. He has been on the staff of that university since 1959, before which date he was, successively, a clerk in the Manchester cotton trade, a wartime soldier, and a schoolmaster. His present research interests concern both social and economic aspects of the Industrial Revolution in Britain. He is author of a number of books on modern British economic history and has contributed many articles to the learned journals.

Everett E. Hagen is Professor of Economics and of Political Science at Massachusetts Institute of Technology, and senior staff member of the Center for International Studies.

He is currently engaged on the preparation of a volume on the economics of development of low-income countries, which will give special emphasis to the process of industrialization.

S. B. Saul, B.Com., Ph.D., has occupied the Chair of Economic History at the University of Edinburgh since 1963, prior to which he taught at the University of Liverpool. He is author of a book on British overseas trade in the period 1870–1914 and of articles on trade and investment, imperialism, and the development of engineering.